Shakespeare Explained

Hamlet

JOSEPH SOBRAN

mc Marshall Cavendish Benchmark
New York

Cover: Mark Rylance played Hamlet in the Royal Shakespeare Company's 1988 production.

Series consultant: Richard Larkin

Marshall Cavendish
99 White Plains Road
Tarrytown, New York 10591
www.marshallcavendish.us

Library of Congress Cataloging-in-Publication Data
Sobran, Joseph.
Hamlet / by Joseph Sobran.
p. cm. — (Shakespeare explained)
Summary: "A literary analysis of the play Hamlet by William Shakespeare. Includes information on the history and culture of Elizabethan England"—Provided by publisher.
Includes bibliographical references and index.
ISBN 978-0-7614-3027-8
1. Shakespeare, William, 1564-1616. Hamlet—Juvenile literature.
2. Shakespeare, William, 1564-1616. Hamlet—Examinations—Study guides. I. Title.
PR2807.S73 2009
822.3'3—dc22
2008007090

Photo research by: Linda Sykes
Robbie Jack/Corbis: front cover; Vasiliy Koval/istockphoto: 1; Neven Mendrila/Shutterstock: 3; Raciro/ istockphoto: 4; 38, 44, 100; Art Parts RF: 6, 8, 13, 24, 25, 32,; Nik Wheeler/Corbis: 11; Portraitgalerie, Schloss Ambras, Innsbruck, Austria/Erich Lessing/Art Resource, NY: 18; AA World Travel Library/Alamy: 20; Hideo Kurihara/Alamy: 22; Corbis Sygma: 27; Andrew Fox/Corbis: 30;The Everett Collection: 37; ART.COM: 43, 99; Ken Welsh/Bridgeman Art Library: 47; T. Charles Erickson: 52; Castle Rock Entertainment/The Kobal Collection: 63; Robbie Jack/Corbis: 69; The Granger Collection: 77, 85; Paramount/The Kobal Collection: 79.

Editor: Deborah Grahame
Publisher: Michelle Bisson
Art Director: Anahid Hamparian
Series Design: Kay Petronio

Printed in: Malaysia

135642

69929
Contents
69929

Shakespeare and His World

WILLIAM SHAKESPEARE, OFTEN NICKNAMED "THE BARD," IS, BEYOND ANY COMPARISON, THE MOST TOWERING NAME IN ENGLISH LITERATURE. MANY CONSIDER HIS PLAYS THE GREATEST EVER WRITTEN. HE STANDS OUT EVEN AMONG GENIUSES.

Yet the Bard is also closer to our hearts than lesser writers, and his tremendous reputation should neither intimidate us nor prevent us from enjoying the simple delights he offers in such abundance. It is as if he had written for each of us personally. As he himself put it, "One touch of nature makes the whole world kin."

Such tragedies as *Hamlet*, *Romeo and Juliet*, and *Macbeth* are world-famous, still performed on stage and in films. These and others have also been adapted for radio, television, opera, ballet, pantomime, novels, comic books, and other media. Two of the best ways to become familiar with them are to watch some of the many fine movies that have been made of them and to listen to recordings of them by some of the world's great actors.

Even Shakespeare's individual characters have a life of their own, like real historical figures. Hamlet is still regarded as the most challenging role ever written for an actor. Roughly as many whole books have been written about Hamlet, an imaginary character, as about actual historical figures such as Abraham Lincoln and Napoleon Bonaparte.

Shakespeare created an amazing variety of vivid characters. One of Shakespeare's most peculiar traits was that he loved his characters so much—even some of his villains and secondary or comic characters—that at times he let them run away with the play, stealing attention from his heroes and heroines.

So in *A Midsummer Night's Dream* audiences remember the absurd and lovable fool Bottom the Weaver better than the lovers who are the main characters. Romeo's friend Mercutio is more fiery and witty than Romeo himself; legend claims that Shakespeare said he had to kill Mercutio or Mercutio would have killed the play.

Shakespeare also wrote dozens of comedies and historical plays, as well as nondramatic poems. Although his tragedies are now regarded as his greatest works, he freely mixed them with comedy and history. And his sonnets are among the supreme love poems in the English language.

It is Shakespeare's mastery of the English language that keeps his words familiar to us today. Every literate person knows dramatic lines such as "Wherefore art thou Romeo?"; "My kingdom for a horse!"; "To be or not to be: that is the question"; "Friends, Romans, countrymen, lend me your ears"; and "What fools these mortals be!" Shakespeare's sonnets are noted for their sweetness: "Shall I compare thee to a summer's day?"

WITHOUT A DOUBT, SHAKESPEARE WAS THE GREATEST MASTER OF THE ENGLISH LANGUAGE WHO EVER LIVED. BUT JUST WHAT DOES THAT MEAN?

Shakespeare's vocabulary was huge, full of references to the Bible as well as Greek and Roman mythology. Yet his most brilliant phrases often combine very simple and familiar words:

"WHAT'S IN A NAME? THAT WHICH WE CALL A ROSE BY ANY OTHER NAME WOULD SMELL AS SWEET."

He has delighted countless millions of readers. And we know him only through his language. He has shaped modern English far more than any other writer.

Or, to put it in more personal terms, you probably quote his words several times every day without realizing it, even if you have never suspected that Shakespeare could be a source of pleasure to you.

So why do so many English-speaking readers find his language so difficult? It is our language, too, but it has changed so much that it is no longer quite the same language—nor a completely different one, either.

Shakespeare's English and ours overlap without being identical. He would have some difficulty understanding us, too! Many of our everyday words and phrases would baffle him.

Shakespeare, for example, would not know what we meant by a *car,* a *radio,* a *movie*, a *television,* a *computer,* or a *sitcom,* since these things did not even exist in his time. Our old-fashioned term *railroad train,* would be unimaginable to him, far in the distant future. We would have to explain to him (if we could) what *nuclear weapons, electricity,* and *democracy* are. He would also be a little puzzled by common expressions such as *high-tech, feel the heat, approval ratings, war criminal, judgmental,* and *whoopie cushion.*

So how can we call him "the greatest master of the English language"? It might seem as if he barely spoke English at all! (He would, however, recognize much of our dirty slang, even if he pronounced it slightly differently. His plays also contain many racial insults to Jews, Africans, Italians, Irish, and others. Today he would be called "insensitive.")

Many of the words of Shakespeare's time have become archaic. Words like *thou, thee, thy, thyself,* and *thine,* which were among the most common words in the language in Shakespeare's day, have all but disappeared today. We simply say *you* for both singular and plural, formal and familiar. Most other modern languages have kept their *thou.*

Sometimes the same words now have different meanings. We are apt to be misled by such simple, familiar words as *kind, wonderful, waste, just,* and *dear,* which he often uses in ways that differ from our usage.

Shakespeare also doesn't always use the words we expect to hear, the words that we ourselves would naturally use. When we might automatically say, "I beg your pardon" or just "Sorry," he might say, "I cry you mercy."

Often a glossary and footnotes will solve all three of these problems for us. But it is most important to bear in mind that Shakespeare was often hard for his first audiences to understand. Even in his own time his rich language was challenging. And this was deliberate. Shakespeare was inventing his own kind of English. It remains unique today.

A child doesn't learn to talk by using a dictionary. Children learn first by sheer immersion. We teach babies by pointing at things and saying their names. Yet the toddler always learns faster than we can teach! Even as babies we are geniuses. Dictionaries can help us later, when we already speak and read the language well (and learn more slowly).

So the best way to learn Shakespeare is not to depend on the footnotes and glossary too much, but instead to be like a baby: just get into the flow of the language. Go to performances of the plays or watch movies of them.

Hundreds of phrases have entered the English language from *Hamlet* alone, including "to hold, as t'were, the mirror up to nature"; "murder most foul"; "the thousand natural shocks that flesh is heir to"; "flaming youth"; "a countenance more in sorrow than in anger"; "the play's the thing"; "neither a borrower nor a lender be"; "in my mind's eye"; "something is rotten in the state of Denmark"; "alas, poor Yorick"; and "the lady doth protest too much, methinks."

From other plays we get the phrases "star-crossed lovers"; "what's in a name?"; "we have scotched the snake, not killed it"; "one fell swoop"; "it was Greek to me;" "I come to bury Caesar, not to praise him"; and "the most unkindest cut of all"—all these are among our household words. In fact, Shakespeare even gave us the expression "household words." No wonder his contemporaries marveled at his "fine filed phrase" and swooned at the "mellifluous and honey-tongued Shakespeare."

Shakespeare's words seem to combine music, magic, wisdom, and humor:

"THE COURSE OF TRUE LOVE NEVER DID RUN SMOOTH."

"HE JESTS AT SCARS THAT NEVER FELT A WOUND."

"THE FAULT, DEAR BRUTUS, IS NOT IN OUR STARS,
BUT IN OURSELVES, THAT WE ARE UNDERLINGS."

"COWARDS DIE MANY TIMES BEFORE THEIR DEATHS;
THE VALIANT NEVER TASTE OF DEATH BUT ONCE."

"NOT THAT I LOVED CAESAR LESS, BUT
THAT I LOVED ROME MORE."

THERE ARE MORE THINGS IN HEAVEN AND EARTH,
HORATIO, THAN ARE DREAMT OF IN YOUR PHILOSOPHY."

"BREVITY IS THE SOUL OF WIT."

"THERE'S A DIVINITY THAT SHAPES OUR ENDS,
ROUGH-HEW THEM HOW WE WILL."

Four centuries after Shakespeare lived, to speak English is to quote him. His huge vocabulary and linguistic fertility are still astonishing. He has had a powerful effect on all of us, whether we realize it or not. We may wonder how it is even possible for a single human being to say so many memorable things.

Only the King James translation of the Bible, perhaps, has had a more profound and pervasive influence on the English language than Shakespeare. And, of course, the Bible was written by many authors over many centuries, and the King James translation, published in 1611, was the combined effort of many scholars.

EARLY LIFE

So who, exactly, was Shakespeare? Mystery surrounds his life, largely because few records were kept during his time. Some people have even doubted his identity, arguing that the real author of Shakespeare's plays must have been a man of superior formal education and wide experience. In a sense such doubts are a natural and understandable reaction to his rare, almost miraculous powers of expression, but some people feel that the doubts themselves show a lack of respect for the supremely human poet.

Most scholars agree that Shakespeare was born in the town of Stratford-upon-Avon in the county of Warwickshire, England, in April 1564. He was baptized, according to local church records, Gulielmus (William) Shakspere (the name was spelled in several different ways) on April 26 of that year. He was one of several children, most of whom died young.

His father, John Shakespeare (or Shakspere), was a glove maker and, at times, a town official. He was often in debt or being fined for unknown delinquencies, perhaps failure to attend church regularly. It is suspected that John was a "recusant" (secret and illegal) Catholic, but there is no

SHAKESPEARE'S CHILDHOOD HOME IS CARED FOR BY AN INDEPENDENT CHARITY, THE SHAKESPEARE BIRTHPLACE TRUST, IN STRATFORD-UPON-AVON, WARWICKSHIRE, ENGLAND.

proof. Many scholars have found Catholic tendencies in Shakespeare's plays, but whether Shakespeare was Catholic or not we can only guess.

At the time of Shakespeare's birth, England was torn by religious controversy and persecution. The country had left the Roman Catholic Church during the reign of King Henry VIII, who had died in 1547. Two of Henry's children, Edward and Mary, ruled after his death. When his daughter Elizabeth I became queen in 1558, she upheld his claim that the monarch of England was also head of the English Church.

Did William attend the local grammar school? He was probably entitled to, given his father's prominence in Stratford, but again, we face a frustrating absence of proof, and many people of the time learned to read very well without schooling. If he went to the town school, he would also have learned the rudiments of Latin.

We know very little about the first half of William's life. In 1582, when he was eighteen, he married Anne Hathaway, eight years his senior. Their first daughter, Susanna, was born six months later. The following year they had twins, Hamnet and Judith.

At this point William disappears from the records again. By the early 1590s we find "William Shakespeare" in London, a member of the city's leading acting company, called the Lord Chamberlain's Men. Many of Shakespeare's greatest roles, we are told, were first performed by the company's star, Richard Burbage.

Curiously, the first work published under (and identified with) Shakespeare's name was not a play but a long erotic poem, *Venus and Adonis*, in 1593. It was dedicated to the young Earl of Southampton, Henry Wriothesley.

Venus and Adonis was a spectacular success, and Shakespeare was immediately hailed as a major poet. In 1594 he dedicated a longer, more serious poem to Southampton, *The Rape of Lucrece*. It was another hit, and for many years, these two poems were considered Shakespeare's greatest works, despite the popularity of his plays.

TODAY MOVIES, NOT LIVE PLAYS, ARE THE MORE POPULAR ART FORM. FORTUNATELY MOST OF SHAKESPEARE'S PLAYS HAVE BEEN FILMED, AND THE BEST OF THESE MOVIES OFFER AN EXCELLENT WAY TO MAKE THE BARD'S ACQUAINTANCE. RECENTLY, KENNETH BRANAGH HAS BECOME A RESPECTED CONVERTER OF SHAKESPEARE'S PLAYS INTO FILM.

Hamlet

Hamlet, Shakespeare's most famous play, has been well filmed several times. In 1948 Laurence Olivier won three Academy Awards—for best picture, best actor, and best director—for his version of the play. The film allowed him to show some of the magnetism that made him famous on the stage. Nobody spoke Shakespeare's lines more thrillingly.

The young Derek Jacobi played Hamlet in a 1980 BBC production of the play, with Patrick Stewart (now best known for *Star Trek, the Next Generation*) as the guilty king. Jacobi, like Olivier, has a gift for speaking the lines freshly; he never seems to be merely reciting the famous and familiar words. But whereas Olivier has animal passion, Jacobi is more intellectual. It is fascinating to compare the ways these two outstanding actors play Shakespeare's most complex character.

Franco Zeffirelli's 1990 *Hamlet*, starring Mel Gibson, is fascinating in a different way. Gibson, of course, is best known as an action hero, and he is not well suited to this supremely witty and introspective role, but Zeffirelli cuts the text drastically, and the result turns *Hamlet* into something that few people would have expected: a short, swift-moving action movie. Several of the other characters are brilliantly played.

Henry IV, Part One

The 1979 BBC Shakespeare series production does a commendable job in this straightforward approach to the play. Battle scenes are effective despite obvious restrictions in an indoor studio setting. Anthony Quayle gives jovial Falstaff a darker edge, and Tim Pigott-Smith's Hotspur is buoyed by some humor. Jon Finch plays King Henry IV with noble authority, and David Gwillim gives Hal a surprisingly successful transformation from boy prince to heir apparent.

Julius Caesar

No really good movie of *Julius Caesar* exists, but the 1953 film, with Marlon Brando as Mark Antony, will do. James Mason is a thoughtful Brutus, and John Gielgud, then ranked with Laurence Olivier among the greatest Shakespearean actors, plays the villainous Cassius. The film is rather dull, and Brando is out of place in a Roman toga, but it is still worth viewing.

Macbeth

Roman Polanski is best known as a director of thrillers and horror films, so it may seem natural that he should have done his 1971 *The Tragedy of Macbeth* as an often-gruesome slasher flick. But this is also one of the most vigorous of all Shakespeare films. Macbeth and his wife are played by Jon Finch and Francesca Annis, neither known for playing Shakespeare, but they are young and attractive in roles that are usually given to older actors, which gives the story a fresh flavor.

The Merchant of Venice

Once again the matchless Sir Laurence Olivier delivers a great performance as Shylock with his wife Joan Plowright as Portia in the 1974 TV film, adapted from the 1970 National Theater (of Britain) production. A 1980 BBC offering features Warren Mitchell as Shylock and Gemma Jones as Portia, with John Rhys-Davies as Salerio. The most recent production, starring Al Pacino as Shylock, Jeremy Irons as Antonio, and Joseph Fiennes as Bassanio, was filmed in Venice and released in 2004.

A Midsummer Night's Dream

Because of the prestige of his tragedies, we tend to forget how many comedies Shakespeare wrote—nearly twice the number of tragedies. Of these perhaps the most popular has always been the enchanting, atmospheric, and very silly masterpiece *A Midsummer Night's Dream.*

In more recent times several films have been made of *A Midsummer Night's Dream.* Among the more notable have been Max Reinhardt's 1935 black-and-white version, with Mickey Rooney (then a child star) as Puck.

Of the several film versions, the one starring Kevin Kline as Bottom and Stanley Tucci as Puck, made in 1999 with nineteenth-century costumes and directed by Michael Hoffman, ranks among the finest, and is surely one of the most sumptuous to watch.

Othello

Orson Welles did a budget European version in 1952, now available as a restored DVD. Laurence Olivier's 1965 film performance is predictably remarkable, though it has been said that he would only approach the part by honoring, even emulating, Paul Robeson's definitive interpretation that ran on Broadway in 1943. (Robeson was the first black actor to play Othello, the Moor of Venice, and he did so to critical acclaim, though sadly his performance was never filmed.) Maggie Smith plays a formidable Desdemona opposite Olivier, and her youth and energy will surprise younger audiences who know her only from the Harry Potter films. Laurence Fishburne brilliantly portrayed Othello in the 1995 film, costarring with Kenneth Branagh as a surprisingly human Iago, though Irène Jacob's Desdemona was disappointingly weak.

Romeo and Juliet

This, the world's most famous love story, has been filmed many times, twice very successfully over the last generation. Franco Zeffirelli directed a hit version in 1968 with Leonard Whiting and the rapturously pretty Olivia Hussey, set in Renaissance Italy. Baz Luhrmann made a much more contemporary version, with a loud rock score, starring Leonardo Di Caprio and Claire Danes, in 1996.

It seems safe to say that Shakespeare would have preferred Zeffirelli's movie, with its superior acting and rich, romantic, sun-drenched Italian scenery.

The Tempest

A 1960 Hallmark Hall of Fame production featured Maurice Evans as Prospero, Lee Remick as Miranda, Roddy McDowall as Ariel, and Richard Burton as Caliban. The special effects are primitive and the costumes are ludicrous, but it moves along at a fast pace. Another TV version aired in 1998 and was nominated for a Golden Globe. Peter Fonda played Gideon Prosper, and Katherine Heigl played his daughter Miranda Prosper. Sci-Fi fans may already know that the classic 1956 film *Forbidden Planet* is modeled on themes and characters from the play.

Twelfth Night

Trevor Nunn adapted the play for the 1996 film he also directed in a rapturous Edwardian setting, with big names like Helena Bonham Carter, Richard E. Grant, Imogen Stubbs, and Ben Kingsley as Feste. A 2003 film set in modern Britain provides an interesting multicultural experience; it features an Anglo-Indian cast with Parminder Nagra (*Bend It Like Beckham*) playing Viola. For the truly intrepid, a twelve-minute silent film made in 1910 does a fine job of capturing the play through visual gags and over-the-top gesturing.

THESE FILMS HAVE BEEN SELECTED FOR SEVERAL QUALITIES: APPEAL AND ACCESSIBILITY TO MODERN AUDIENCES, EXCELLENCE IN ACTING, PACING, VISUAL BEAUTY, AND, OF COURSE, FIDELITY TO SHAKESPEARE. THEY ARE THE MOTION PICTURES WE JUDGE MOST LIKELY TO HELP STUDENTS UNDERSTAND THE SOURCE OF THE BARD'S LASTING POWER.

SHAKESPEARE'S THEATER

Today we sometimes speak of "live entertainment." In Shakespeare's day, of course, all entertainment was live, because recordings, films, television, and radio did not yet exist. Even printed books were a novelty.

In fact, most communication in those days was difficult. Transportation was not only difficult but slow, chiefly by horse and boat. Most people were illiterate peasants who lived on farms that they seldom left; cities grew up along waterways and were subject to frequent plagues that could wipe out much of the population within weeks.

Money—in coin form, not paper—was scarce and hardly existed outside the cities. By today's standards, even the rich were poor. Life was precarious. Most children died young, and famine or disease might kill anyone at any time. Everyone was familiar with death. Starvation was not rare or remote, as it is to most of us today. Medical care was poor and might kill as many people as it healed.

This was the grim background of Shakespeare's theater during the reign of Queen Elizabeth I, who ruled from 1558 until her death in 1603. During that period England was also torn by religious conflict, often violent, among Roman Catholics who were

ELIZABETH I, A GREAT PATRON OF POETRY AND THE THEATER, WROTE SONNETS AND TRANSLATED CLASSIC WORKS.

loyal to the Pope, adherents of the Church of England who were loyal to the queen, and the Puritans who would take over the country in the revolution of 1642.

Under these conditions, most forms of entertainment were luxuries that were out of most people's reach. The only way to hear music was to be in the actual physical presence of singers or musicians with their instruments, which were primitive by our standards.

One brutal form of entertainment, popular in London, was bear-baiting. A bear was blinded and chained to a stake, where fierce dogs called mastiffs were turned loose to tear him apart. The theaters had to compete with the bear gardens, as they were called, for spectators.

The Puritans, or radical Protestants, objected to bear-baiting and tried to ban it. Despite their modern reputation, the Puritans were anything but conservative. Conservative people, attached to old customs, hated them. They seemed to upset everything. (Many of America's first settlers, such as the Pilgrims who came over on the *Mayflower*, were dissidents who were fleeing the Church of England.)

Plays were extremely popular, but they were primitive, too. They had to be performed outdoors in the afternoon because of the lack of indoor lighting. Often the "theater" was only an enclosed courtyard. Probably the versions of Shakespeare's plays that we know today were not used in full, but shortened to about two hours for actual performance.

But eventually more regular theaters were built, featuring a raised stage extending into the audience. Poorer spectators (illiterate "groundlings") stood on the ground around it, at times exposed to rain and snow. Wealthier people sat in raised tiers above. Aside from some costumes, there were few props or special effects and almost no scenery. Much had to be imagined: Whole battles might be represented by a few actors with swords. Thunder might be simulated by rattling a sheet of tin offstage.

The plays were far from realistic and, under the conditions of the time, could hardly try to be. Above the rear of the main stage was a small balcony. (It was this balcony from which Juliet spoke to Romeo.) Ghosts and witches might appear by entering through a trapdoor in the stage floor.

Unlike the modern theater, Shakespeare's Globe Theater—he describes it as "this wooden O"—had no curtain separating the stage from the audience. This allowed intimacy between the players and the spectators.

THE RECONSTRUCTED GLOBE THEATER WAS COMPLETED IN 1997 AND IS LOCATED IN LONDON, JUST 200 YARDS (183 METERS) FROM THE SITE OF THE ORIGINAL.

THE SLINGS AND ARROWS OF OUTRAGEOUS FORTUNE

The spectators probably reacted rowdily to the play, not listening in reverent silence. After all they had come to have fun! And few of them were scholars. Again, a play had to amuse people who could not read.

The lines of plays were written and spoken in prose or, more often, in a form of verse called iambic pentameter (ten syllables with five stresses per line). There was no attempt at modern realism. Only males were allowed on the stage, so some of the greatest women's roles ever written had to be played by boys or men. (The same is true, by the way, of the ancient Greek theater.)

Actors had to be versatile, skilled not only in acting, but also in fencing, singing, dancing, and acrobatics. Within its limitations, the theater offered a considerable variety of spectacles.

Plays were big business, not yet regarded as high art, sponsored by important and powerful people (the queen loved them as much as the groundlings did). The London acting companies also toured and performed in the provinces. When plagues struck London, the government might order the theaters to be closed to prevent the spread of disease among crowds. (They remained empty for nearly two years from 1593 to 1594.)

As the theater became more popular, the Puritans grew as hostile to it as they were to bear-baiting. Plays, like books, were censored by the government, and the Puritans fought to increase restrictions, eventually banning any mention of God and other sacred topics on the stage.

In 1642 the Puritans shut down all the theaters in London, and in 1644 they had the Globe demolished. The theaters remained closed until Charles's son King Charles II was restored to the throne in 1660 and the hated Puritans were finally vanquished.

But, by then, the tradition of Shakespeare's theater had been fatally interrupted. His plays remained popular, but they were often rewritten by inferior dramatists and it was many years before they were performed (again) as he had originally written them.

THE ROYAL SHAKESPEARE THEATER, IN STRATFORD-UPON-AVON, WAS CLOSED IN 2007. A NEWLY DESIGNED INTERIOR WITH A 1000-SEAT AUDITORIUM WILL BE COMPLETED IN 2010.

Today, of course, the plays are performed both in theaters and in films, sometimes in costumes of the period (ancient Rome for *Julius Caesar*, medieval England for *Henry V*), sometimes in modern dress (*Richard III* has recently been reset in England in the 1930s).

PLAYS

In the England of Queen Elizabeth I, plays were enjoyed by all classes of people, but they were not yet respected as a serious form of art.

Shakespeare's plays began to appear in print in individual, or "quarto," editions in 1594, but none of these bore his name until 1598. Although his tragedies are now ranked as his supreme achievements, his name was first associated with comedies and with plays about English history.

The dates of Shakespeare's plays are notoriously hard to determine. Few performances of them were documented; some were not printed until decades after they first appeared on the stage. Mainstream scholars generally place most of the comedies and histories in the 1590s, admitting that this time frame is no more than a widely accepted estimate.

The three parts of *King Henry VI*, culminating in a fourth part, *Richard III*, deal with the long and complex dynastic struggle or civil wars known as the Wars of the Roses (1455–1487), one of England's most turbulent periods. Today it is not easy to follow the plots of these plays.

It may seem strange to us that a young playwright should have written such demanding works early in his career, but they were evidently very popular with the Elizabethan public. Of the four, only *Richard III*, with its wonderfully villainous starring role, is still often performed.

Even today, one of Shakespeare's early comedies, *The Taming of the Shrew*, remains a crowd-pleaser. (It has enjoyed success in a 1999 film adaptation, *10 Things I Hate About You*, with Heath Ledger and Julia Stiles.)

AROUND 1850 DOUBTS STARTED TO SURFACE ABOUT WHO HAD ACTUALLY WRITTEN SHAKESPEARE'S PLAYS, CHIEFLY BECAUSE MANY OTHER AUTHORS, SUCH AS MARK TWAIN, THOUGHT THE PLAYS' AUTHOR WAS TOO WELL EDUCATED AND KNOWLEDGEABLE TO HAVE BEEN THE MODESTLY SCHOOLED MAN FROM STRATFORD.

Who, then, was the real author? Many answers have been given, but the three leading candidates are Francis Bacon, Christopher Marlowe, and Edward de Vere, Earl of Oxford.

Francis Bacon (1561–1626)

Bacon was a distinguished lawyer, scientist, philosopher, and essayist. Many considered him one of the great geniuses of his time, capable of any literary achievement, though he wrote little poetry and, as far as we know, no dramas. When people began to suspect that "Shakespeare" was only a pen name, he seemed like a natural candidate. But his writing style was vastly different from the style of the plays.

Christopher Marlowe (1564–1593)

Marlowe wrote several excellent tragedies in a style much like that of the Shakespeare tragedies, though without the comic blend. But he was reportedly killed in a mysterious incident in 1593, before most of the Bard's plays existed. Could his death have been faked? Is it possible that he lived on for decades in hiding, writing under a pen name? This is what his advocates contend.

Edward de Vere, Earl of Oxford (1550–1604)

Oxford is now the most popular and plausible alternative to the lad from Stratford. He had a high reputation as a poet and playwright in his day, but his life was full of scandal. That controversial life seems to match what the poet says about himself in the sonnets, as well as many events in the plays (especially *Hamlet*). However, he died in 1604, and most scholars believe this rules him out as the author of plays that were published after that date.

THE GREAT MAJORITY OF EXPERTS REJECT THESE AND ALL OTHER ALTERNATIVE CANDIDATES, STICKING WITH THE TRADITIONAL VIEW, AFFIRMED IN THE 1623 FIRST FOLIO OF THE PLAYS, THAT THE AUTHOR WAS THE MAN FROM STRATFORD. THAT REMAINS THE SAFEST POSITION TO TAKE, UNLESS STARTLING NEW EVIDENCE TURNS UP, WHICH, AT THIS LATE DATE, SEEMS HIGHLY UNLIKELY.

The story is simple: The enterprising Petruchio resolves to marry a rich young woman, Katherina Minola, for her wealth, despite her reputation for having a bad temper. Nothing she does can discourage this dauntless suitor, and the play ends with Kate becoming a submissive wife. It is all the funnier for being unbelievable.

With *Romeo and Juliet* the Bard created his first enduring triumph. This tragedy of "star-crossed lovers" from feuding families is known around the world. Even people with only the vaguest knowledge of Shakespeare are often aware of this universally beloved story. It has inspired countless similar stories and adaptations, such as the hit musical *West Side Story*.

By the mid-1590s Shakespeare was successful and prosperous, a partner in the Lord Chamberlain's Men. He was rich enough to buy New Place, one of the largest houses in his hometown of Stratford.

Yet, at the peak of his good fortune, came the worst sorrow of his life: Hamnet, his only son, died in August 1596 at the age of eleven, leaving nobody to carry on his family name, which was to die out with his two daughters.

Our only evidence of his son's death is a single line in the parish burial register. As far as we know, this crushing loss left no mark on Shakespeare's work. As far as his creative life shows, it was as if nothing had happened. His silence about his grief may be the greatest puzzle of his mysterious life, although, as we shall see, others remain.

During this period, according to traditional dating (even if it must be somewhat hypothetical), came the torrent of Shakespeare's mightiest works. Among these was another quartet of English history plays, this one centering on the legendary King Henry IV, including *Richard II* and the two parts of *Henry IV*.

Then came a series of wonderful romantic comedies: *Much Ado About Nothing*, *As You Like It*, and *Twelfth Night*.

ACTOR JOSEPH FIENNES PORTRAYED THE BARD IN THE 1998 FILM *SHAKESPEARE IN LOVE*, DIRECTED BY JOHN MADDEN.

In 1598 the clergyman Francis Meres, as part of a larger work, hailed Shakespeare as the English Ovid, supreme in love poetry as well as drama. "The Muses would speak with Shakespeare's fine filed phrase," Meres wrote, "if they would speak English." He added praise of Shakespeare's "sugared sonnets among his private friends." It is tantalizing; Meres seems to know something of the poet's personal life, but he gives us no hard information. No wonder biographers are frustrated.

Next the Bard returned gloriously to tragedy with *Julius Caesar*. In the play Caesar has returned to Rome in great popularity after his military triumphs.

Brutus and several other leading senators, suspecting that Caesar means to make himself king, plot to assassinate him. Midway through the play, after the assassination, comes one of Shakespeare's most famous scenes. Brutus speaks at Caesar's funeral. But then Caesar's friend Mark Antony delivers a powerful attack on the conspirators, inciting the mob to fury. Brutus and the others, forced to flee Rome, die in the ensuing civil war. In the end the spirit of Caesar wins after all. If Shakespeare had written nothing after *Julius Caesar*, he would still have been remembered as one of the greatest playwrights of all time. But his supreme works were still to come.

Only Shakespeare could have surpassed *Julius Caesar*, and he did so with *Hamlet* (usually dated about 1600). King Hamlet of Denmark has died, apparently bitten by a poisonous snake. Claudius, his brother, has married the dead king's widow, Gertrude, and become the new king, to the disgust and horror of Prince Hamlet. The ghost of old Hamlet appears to young Hamlet, reveals that he was actually poisoned by Claudius, and demands revenge. Hamlet accepts this as his duty, but cannot bring himself to kill his hated uncle. What follows is Shakespeare's most brilliant and controversial plot.

The story of *Hamlet* is set against the religious controversies of the Bard's time. Is the ghost in hell or purgatory? Is Hamlet Catholic or Protestant? Can revenge ever be justified? We are never really given the answers to such questions. But the play reverberates with them.

THE KING'S MEN

In 1603 Queen Elizabeth I died, and King James VI of Scotland became King James I of England. He also became the patron of Shakespeare's acting company, so the Lord Chamberlain's Men became the King's Men. From this point on, we know less of Shakespeare's life in London than in Stratford, where he kept acquiring property.

In the later years of the sixteenth century Shakespeare had been a rather elusive figure in London, delinquent in paying taxes. From 1602 to 1604 he lived, according to his own later testimony, with a French immigrant family named Mountjoy. After 1604 there is no record of any London residence for Shakespeare, nor do we have any reliable recollection of him or his whereabouts by others. As always, the documents leave much to be desired.

Nearly as great as *Hamlet* is *Othello*, and many regard *King Lear*, the heart-breaking tragedy about an old king and his three daughters, as Shakespeare's supreme tragedy. Shakespeare's shortest tragedy, *Macbeth*, tells the story of a Scottish lord and his wife who plot to murder the king of Scotland to gain the throne for themselves. *Antony and Cleopatra*, a sequel to *Julius Caesar*, depicts the aging Mark Antony in love with the enchanting queen of Egypt. *Coriolanus*, another Roman tragedy, is the poet's least popular masterpiece.

SONNETS AND THE END

The year 1609 saw the publication of Shakespeare's sonnets. Of these 154 puzzling love poems, the first 126 are addressed to a handsome young man, unnamed, but widely believed to be the Earl of Southampton; the rest concern a dark woman, also unidentified. These mysteries are still debated by scholars.

Near the end of his career Shakespeare turned to comedy again, but it was a comedy of a new and more serious kind. Magic plays a large role in these late plays. For example, in *The Tempest*, the exiled duke of Milan, Prospero, uses magic to defeat his enemies and bring about a final reconciliation.

According to the most commonly accepted view, Shakespeare, not yet fifty, retired to Stratford around 1610. He died prosperous in 1616, and left a will that divided his goods, with a famous provision leaving his wife "my second-best bed." He was buried in the chancel of the parish church, under a tombstone bearing a crude rhyme:

> GOOD FRIEND, FOR JESUS SAKE FORBEARE
> TO DIG THE DUST ENCLOSED HERE.
> BLEST BE THE MAN THAT SPARES THESE STONES,
> AND CURSED BE HE THAT MOVES MY BONES.

This epitaph is another hotly debated mystery: Did the great poet actually compose these lines himself?

SHAKESPEARE'S GRAVE IN HOLY TRINITY CHURCH, STRATFORD-UPON-AVON. HIS WIFE, ANNE HATHAWAY, IS BURIED BESIDE HIM.

THE FOLIO

In 1623 Shakespeare's colleagues of the King's Men produced a large volume of the plays (excluding the sonnets and other poems) titled *The Comedies, Histories, and Tragedies of Mr. William Shakespeare* with a woodcut portrait—the only known portrait—of the Bard. As a literary monument it is priceless, containing our only texts of half the plays; as a source of biographical information it is severely disappointing, giving not even the dates of Shakespeare's birth and death.

Ben Jonson, then England's poet laureate, supplied a long prefatory poem saluting Shakespeare as the equal of the great classical Greek tragedians Aeschylus, Sophocles, and Euripides, adding that "He was not of an age, but for all time."

Some would later denigrate Shakespeare. His reputation took more than a century to conquer Europe, where many regarded him as semi-barbarous. His works were not translated before 1740. Jonson himself, despite his personal affection, would deprecate "idolatry" of the Bard. For a time Jonson himself was considered more "correct" than Shakespeare, and possibly the superior artist.

But Jonson's generous verdict is now the whole world's. Shakespeare was not merely of his own age, "but for all time."

allegory—a story in which characters and events stand for general moral truths. Shakespeare never uses this form simply, but his plays are full of allegorical elements.

alliteration—repetition of one or more initial sounds, especially consonants, as in the saying "through thick and thin," or in Julius Caesar's statement, "veni, vidi, vici."

allusion—a reference, especially when the subject referred to is not actually named, but is unmistakably hinted at.

aside—a short speech in which a character speaks to the audience, unheard by other characters on the stage.

comedy—a story written to amuse, using devices such as witty dialogue (high comedy) or silly physical movement (low comedy). Most of Shakespeare's comedies were romantic comedies, incorporating lovers who endure separations, misunderstandings, and other obstacles but who are finally united in a happy resolution.

deus ex machine—an unexpected, artificial resolution to a play's convoluted plot. Literally, "god out of a machine."

dialogue—speech that takes place among two or more characters.

diction—choice of words for tone. A speech's diction may be dignified (as when a king formally addresses his court), comic (as when the ignorant gravediggers debate whether Ophelia deserves a religious funeral), vulgar, romantic, or whatever the dramatic occasion requires. Shakespeare was a master of diction.

Elizabethan—having to do with the reign of Queen Elizabeth I, from 1558 until her death in 1603. This is considered the most famous period in the history of England, chiefly because of Shakespeare and other noted authors (among them Sir Philip Sidney, Edmund Spenser, and Christopher Marlowe). It was also an era of military glory, especially the defeat of the huge Spanish Armada in 1588.

Globe—the Globe Theater housed Shakespeare's acting company, the Lord Chamberlain's Men (later known as the King's Men). Built in 1598, it caught fire and burned down during a performance of *Henry VIII* in 1613.

hyperbole—an excessively elaborate exaggeration used to create special emphasis or a comic effect, as in Montague's remark that his son Romeo's sighs are "adding to clouds more clouds" in *Romeo and Juliet*.

irony—a discrepancy between what a character says and what he or she truly believes, what is expected to happen and what really happens, or between what a character says and what others understand.

metaphor—a figure of speech in which one thing is identified with another, such as when Hamlet calls his father a "fair mountain." (See also ***simile***.)

monologue—a speech delivered by a single character.

motif—a recurrent theme or image, such as disease in *Hamlet* or moonlight in *A Midsummer Night's Dream*.

oxymoron—a phrase that combines two contradictory terms, as in the phrase "sounds of silence" or Hamlet's remark, "I must be cruel only to be kind."

personification—imparting personality to something impersonal ("the sky wept"); giving human qualities to an idea or an inanimate object, as in the saying "love is blind."

pun—a playful treatment of words that sound alike, or are exactly the same, but have different meanings. In *Romeo and Juliet* Mercutio says, after being fatally wounded, "Ask for me tomorrow and you shall find me a grave man." "Grave" could mean either a place of burial or serious.

simile—a figure of speech in which one thing is compared to another, usually using the word *like* or *as*. (See also ***metaphor***.)

soliloquy—a speech delivered by a single character, addressed to the audience. The most famous are those of Hamlet, but Shakespeare uses this device frequently to tell us his characters' inner thoughts.

symbol—a visible thing that stands for an invisible quality, as poison in *Hamlet* stands for evil and treachery.

syntax—sentence structure or grammar. Shakespeare displays amazing variety of syntax, from the sweet simplicity of his songs to the clotted fury of his great tragic heroes, who can be very difficult to understand at a first hearing. These effects are deliberate; if we are confused, it is because Shakespeare means to confuse us.

theme—the abstract subject or message of a work of art, such as revenge in *Hamlet* or overweening ambition in *Macbeth*.

tone—the style or approach of a work of art. The tone of *A Midsummer Night's Dream*, set by the lovers, Bottom's crew, and the fairies, is light and sweet. The tone of *Macbeth*, set by the witches, is dark and sinister.

tragedy—a story that traces a character's fall from power, sanity, or privilege. Shakespeare's well-known tragedies include *Hamlet, Macbeth,* and *Othello*.

tragicomedy—a story that combines elements of both tragedy and comedy, moving a heavy plot through twists and turns to a happy ending.

verisimilitude—having the appearance of being real or true.

understatement—a statement expressing less than intended, often with an ironic or comic intention; the opposite of hyperbole.

SHAKESPEARE AND *HAMLET*

A movie poster for the 1948 ▶ film starring and directed by Laurence Olivier

Chapter One

CHAPTER ONE

Shakespeare and Hamlet

THE TRAGEDY OF HAMLET, PRINCE OF DENMARK, USUALLY DATED AROUND 1600, IS BY FAR THE MOST FAMOUS PLAY EVER WRITTEN, THE MOST OFTEN PERFORMED ON THE STAGE, FILMED, QUOTED, STUDIED, DEBATED, AND WRITTEN ABOUT. IT HAS BEEN THE SUBJECT OF THOUSANDS OF BOOKS AND ARTICLES. THE SOMETIMES VIOLENT BUT SUPREMELY ELOQUENT ROLE OF HAMLET HIMSELF IS THE MOST CHALLENGING EVER WRITTEN FOR ANY ACTOR, AND NEARLY EVERY GREAT STAGE ACTOR HAS PLAYED IT.

Beyond comparison the most popular and controversial play of all time, *Hamlet* had its origins in an obscure, and very crude, legend of a Danish prince avenging his father's murder by his uncle, who marries his mother and becomes king. Whether it has any basis in fact is unknowable, but it hardly matters. Shakespeare sets his play in the sixteenth century of the Christian era, during the time of the Reformation. The reader should have a basic knowledge of the Bible and, if possible, of both Catholic and Protestant doctrine, especially on matters such as the sacraments and purgatory.

By about 1576 a French chronicler named François de Belleforest had written a version of it in which the prince, Amleth, pretends he is mad in order to avert his uncle's suspicion that he is plotting revenge. There is no ghost to tell Amleth the king had been murdered; the murder occurs openly, at a banquet. Amleth foils his uncle's attempts to spy on him. One of the agents is a girl, who falls in love with Amleth and protects him from the uncle. Another is a counselor, whom Amleth kills and cuts to pieces when he catches him spying on Amleth and his mother. (Amleth then feeds the pieces of the corpse to swine.)

The story continues episodically, with Amleth finally killing his uncle and his entire court by starting a fire at another banquet; he himself survives, becomes a great warrior, marries a princess, and dies in battle years later. This saga has little in common with the play that Shakespeare would make from its bare outline: The brutal Amleth is not given to philosophical soliloquies.

"O THAT THIS TOO TOO SOLID FLESH WOULD MELT"

Most scholars date Shakespeare's tragedy to about 1600; they explain references to a *Hamlet* play in 1589, 1594, and 1596 by suggesting that there was an earlier play by that name, which they have dubbed the *Ur-Hamlet* and assume was the immediate source of Shakespeare's masterpiece. But this is sheer speculation; no positive evidence proves that such a play ever existed. No author was named, and no text of it has survived. Still the idea of the play *Ur-Hamlet* has become dogma in Shakespeare scholarship.

The mystery of *Hamlet* is deepened by another curious fact: We possess three distinct versions of the play's text. One is the very short "bad" quarto (or small individual edition) of 1603; another is the much longer "good" quarto of 1604; the third is the version published in the great folio of the plays in 1623, which is nearly identical to the "good" quarto. (It deletes about 200 lines from the 1604 copy and adds about 70 new ones. Most modern editions, including this one, combine the 1604 and 1623 texts.)

The "bad" quarto appears to be an actor's botched attempt to reconstruct the play from memory; it is mostly a mess, comically botching the play's most famous speeches. Hamlet's great soliloquy, for instance, begins like this:

TO BE, OR NOT TO BE, AYE, THERE'S THE POINT:
TO DIE, TO SLEEP; IS THAT ALL? AYE, ALL.
NO, TO SLEEP, TO DREAM, AYE, MARRY THERE IT GOES,
FOR IN THAT SLEEP OF DEATH, WHEN WE AWAKE,
AND BORNE BEFORE AN EVERLASTING JUDGE,
FROM WHENCE NO PASSENGER EVER RETURNED,
THE UNDISCOVERED COUNTRY, AT WHOSE SIGHT
THE HAPPY SMILE, AND THE ACCURSED DAMNED.

"SOMETHING IS ROTTEN IN THE STATE OF DENMARK"

And so on. It sounds pathetic, but the "bad" quarto (only two copies of it exist, both of them mutilated) tells us that the play was very popular by 1603 and had been widely performed—in London, at the universities at Oxford and Cambridge, "and elsewhere." A few other references confirm its wide appeal; it "please[d] all," one writer observed. It was even performed aboard a ship off the coast of Africa in 1607 and 1608, and in Germany not long afterward. The demand for it was such that the Belleforest tale was translated into English in 1608, with the character Amleth becoming "Hamblet."

The student need not be distracted by all these details that vex the specialists, but it is a good idea to be aware that *Hamlet* has been problematic in many respects.

THE PLAY'S THE THING

- OVERVIEW AND ANALYSIS
- LIST OF MAJOR CHARACTERS
- ANALYSIS OF MAJOR CHARACTERS

A lobby card of the Warner Brothers' 1990 film directed by Franco Zeffirelli ▶

Chapter Two

CHAPTER TWO

The Play's the Thing

ACT I, SCENE 1

OVERVIEW

It is a bitterly cold midnight on the ramparts of the king's castle at Elsinore in Denmark. The sentinel Francisco is relieved by another, Barnardo. Marcellus is coming, too, and he will bring with him the scholar Horatio, who does not believe what these men say—that they have seen on the previous two nights a sinister ghost that looks exactly like the dead King Hamlet. They hope Horatio will not only see the Ghost but get it to speak.

Suddenly the Ghost appears, wearing armor. Horatio orders it to speak to him, but when it seems about to, it says nothing and marches away as if offended.

After the Ghost has gone, the three men speculate on what its appearance may mean. Denmark is feverishly preparing for war with Norway. Horatio recalls that old King Hamlet had been dared to engage in single combat by King Fortinbras of Norway, each wagering a certain amount of land on the outcome. Hamlet had won, slaying Fortinbras; now young Fortinbras, the dead king's son, has raised an army and seeks to recover the lands his father lost. (The name *Fortinbras* means "strong arm.") Horatio thinks this may somehow explain why the Ghost is appearing now.

During these speculations the Ghost returns. Again Horatio tells it to explain itself and it seems about to speak when the cock crows, whereupon it departs "like a guilty thing/Upon a fearful summons."

As dawn breaks Marcellus mentions the legend that ghosts cannot appear to men during the Christmas season, when the nights are wholesome and fairies and witches are powerless. Horatio says he believes this "in part," and urges that they report the Ghost's appearance to young Prince Hamlet; surely it will speak to him! The others agree, and Marcellus knows where they will find Hamlet this morning.

ANALYSIS

This scene is a masterpiece of drama and exposition. Within barely fifty lines Shakespeare creates terrific dramatic tension. The entire scene, in less than two hundred lines, takes us plausibly from midnight to dawn. Shakespeare manipulates our sense of time with astounding skill.

Throughout the scene the Ghost is ambiguous but menacing, "a guilty thing" that is "fair" yet "warlike" in form. It shuns the daylight. What can it mean?

ACT I, SCENE 2

OVERVIEW

As the day continues Denmark's new king, Claudius, is addressing his court at Elsinore. His brother Hamlet has recently died; he has married the widow, Queen Gertrude, and assumed the throne. He thanks the dignitaries for their support in all this.

Turning to foreign matters, he notes that young Fortinbras is threatening to invade Denmark with his army to regain those lands his father lost to the old King Hamlet. Claudius sends two diplomats, Cornelius and Voltemand, to Norway to ask the ailing old king to control his nephew.

While they are gone Claudius turns to young Laertes, son of his chief counselor, Polonius, to ask about a request he has mentioned. Laertes says he would like permission to return to Paris, from which he has come to witness Claudius's coronation. When Polonius nods his reluctant approval, the king grants his wish.

Now Claudius turns to his nephew Hamlet, who is still wearing black, in mourning for his father. Claudius asks why Hamlet is taking his father's passing so hard; Hamlet answers with bitter sarcasm: "I am too much in the sun" (note the pun on "son").

Hamlet's mother, Gertrude, asks the same question, since death is every human being's common lot. When Hamlet agrees that death is "common," she asks why, then, it "seems" so "particular" with him. He retorts that it not only "seems," it really "is" ("I know not 'seems'"). The depth of his grief is far deeper than externals such as his "inky cloak" and his tears and sighs, "For they are actions that a man might play."

Professing love for Hamlet as his "son" and heir to the throne of Denmark, Claudius reminds Hamlet that every father dies eventually, and chides Hamlet for his prolonged grieving. He especially hopes Hamlet will

KRONBORG CASTLE IN ELSINORE, DENMARK, THE SETTING FOR *HAMLET*, WAS BUILT BETWEEN 1577 AND 1588 BY FREDERICK II.

not go back to school in Wittenberg. Claudius fears Hamlet and wants him to stay in Elsinore where he can watch him.

Hamlet ignores this appeal, but when Gertrude makes the same plea, he sulkily agrees. The king, queen, and other courtiers leave him alone, and he delivers his first great soliloquy: "O that this too too solid Flesh would melt. . . ."

Hamlet is nearly suicidal; he wishes that God had not condemned "self-slaughter." He is distraught not only over his father's death, which he could have handled, but especially over his mother's hasty, incestuous marriage to a man he regards as contemptible: "My father's brother, but no more like my father/Than I to Hercules."

He is heartbroken, but his mood brightens as soon as he recognizes an old friend: his fellow-student Horatio (accompanied by Marcellus and Barnardo). He asks why Horatio has come all the way from Wittenberg. Horatio replies: "My lord, I came to see your father's funeral." With the quick wit we have already seen, Hamlet retorts, "I pray thee, do not mock me, fellow-student;/ I think it was to see my mother's wedding." True, Horatio admits; the marriage closely followed the funeral. It was "thrift," Hamlet quips; so that the meats baked for the funeral could serve as cold cuts for the marriage festivities.

When Hamlet recalls his father, Horatio gets to the point of his visit: "I think I saw him yesternight." He describes the Ghost and its effect on his terrified companions, who were "distilled/Almost to jelly with the act of fear." He is sure that the Ghost will come again tonight. Hamlet resolves to join them on the sentries' platform before midnight; and he will speak to the Ghost himself, no matter what the risk. He suspects that it is coming to speak of "foul play."

ANALYSIS

Claudius is settling into his new role as king with finesse and aplomb. He suavely addresses several problems that confront him, asserting his authority with ease: first, his kingship itself, with his somewhat dubious marriage to his brother's widow; second, the threat from young Fortinbras of Norway; third, Laertes's eagerness to return to France; and finally, his disgruntled nephew Hamlet's prolonged mourning for his dead father (and his bitter rejection of Claudius's new order). Hamlet's first soliloquy reveals the depth of his discontent: It verges on the suicidal.

This scene once again displays Shakespeare's mastery of exposition. He conveys a remarkable amount of information with extreme economy, laying the groundwork for the whole tragedy. The university at Wittenberg, site of the new Protestant movement and much religious controversy, is mentioned four times within a few lines. The play never mentions it again, but this is enough to tell us (and a literate Elizabethan spectator) that Hamlet is aware of the great theological disputes of his day, toward which the play seems, on the surface at least, carefully noncommittal.

The suspense about the Ghost's meaning and purpose—and, in fact, its very nature—continues to build. Hamlet will get some answers when he speaks to it tonight—or so we hope.

ACT I, SCENE 3

OVERVIEW

Later that day Laertes is about to sail for France. But before he leaves he warns his sister Ophelia to beware of Hamlet, who, being a prince, may be free to compromise her sexually and ruin her honor. Even if Hamlet sincerely loves her now, he is young and may change his mind. Ophelia listens, but teases her brother by telling him that he had better behave himself in France and practice the virtues he preaches!

Polonius comes to say good-bye to his son, adding some "precepts" on wise behavior. He counsels thrift, moderation, prudence, and so forth.

Once Laertes is gone, Polonius also warns Ophelia against Hamlet. He is even more cynical than his son; he thinks Hamlet's interest in Ophelia is purely sexual, and he bluntly orders her to have nothing more to do with that. She meekly promises to obey.

ANALYSIS

Polonius's precepts to Laertes all sound sensible, but they show Polonius to be almost Hamlet's opposite: a man who prizes thrift, caution, and safety above everything else. He cares nothing for nobility of soul or other purely moral qualities. It is instructive to contrast his advice to Laertes with Hamlet's generous praise of Horatio in Act III, Scene 2.

He is even more narrow-minded in his orders to Ophelia. He is strict because he is suspicious; he has no faith in either his daughter or Hamlet. She, on the other hand, recognizes that Hamlet is "honorable" in his vows of love, and her father's command to avoid him crushes her spirit.

This scene also prepares us for what is to come. Polonius is a tyrannical father and a windbag. Later he will be Hamlet's antagonist, far out of his depth with both the prince and the king. His limitations will prove disastrous for himself and others.

ACT I, SCENE 4

OVERVIEW

As agreed, Hamlet meets Horatio and Marcellus on the sentries' platform near midnight the same day to await the Ghost. They hear the sound of drums and cannons in the castle below. Hamlet explains that the king is up late carousing, and these noises accompany his drinking and revelry. This is an old Danish custom, he says, "a custom/More honored in the breach than in the observance," since it has given the Danes a reputation for drunkenness, obscuring their real virtues. The same is true of individuals, he reflects: A single vice may blind the world to all their good qualities.

These thoughts are interrupted by the appearance of the Ghost. Hamlet immediately speaks to it. Unsure whether it is "a spirit of health" or a "goblin damned," he greets it as his father and begs it to say something to him.

When the Ghost beckons Hamlet to follow, Horatio and Marcellus warn Hamlet not to. The Ghost may lead him over a cliff or draw him into madness; who knows what it may do? But Hamlet insists on following the Ghost, saying:

> I DO NOT SET MY LIFE AT A PIN'S FEE;
> AND FOR MY SOUL, WHAT CAN IT DO TO THAT,
> BEING A THING IMMORTAL AS ITSELF?

When Horatio and Marcellus try to hold Hamlet back, Hamlet orders them to let go, or he will "make a ghost" of whoever lays hands on him. (Even in moments of danger, Hamlet's wit never deserts him.)

The two men, fearing for Hamlet, follow at a distance. Marcellus says darkly, "Something is rotten in the state of Denmark." But Horatio has faith, saying, "Heaven will direct it." Marcellus is not so sure.

HAMLET (TY MAYBERRY) ENCOUNTERS THE GHOST (JAMES BLACK) IN A 2003 PRODUCTION AT HOUSTON'S ALLEY THEATER.

ANALYSIS

The first time we see Hamlet presented with a crisis, he shows courage, purpose, and presence of mind. He is a commanding personality. The defiance he showed Claudius earlier was similar to his instant readiness to confront the dreadful Ghost, even if it is a "goblin damned." His friends fear that he may be *too* courageous, considering the dangers they apprehend. But as he says, "My fate cries out."

Later Hamlet will accuse himself of cowardice, but surely that is never his problem, except in his own imagination. Whatever Hamlet's flaws, timidity is not one of them. He is bold to a fault.

The Ghost has not yet revealed its true nature, but up to this point, it has been a foreboding figure, appearing only at night and seeming "warlike," "guilty," and terrifying.

ACT I, SCENE 5

OVERVIEW

Immediately thereafter, at another spot on the castle walls, Hamlet tells the Ghost to stop and speak; he refuses to follow it any farther. It tells him that it must soon give itself up to "sulphurous and tormenting flames." When Hamlet commiserates, "Alas, poor ghost!" it replies sternly, "Pity me not." And it demands revenge:

> I AM THY FATHER'S SPIRIT,
> DOOMED FOR A CERTAIN TERM TO WALK THE NIGHT,
> AND FOR THE DAY CONFINED TO FAST IN FIRES,
> TILL THE FOUL CRIMES DONE IN MY DAYS OF NATURE
> ARE BURNT AND PURGED AWAY.

It says that a full description of its sufferings would freeze Hamlet's blood and make his hair stand on end. Then it asks Hamlet, through his love as a son, to "Revenge [my] foul and most unnatural murder." Hamlet cries:

> HASTE ME TO KNOW'T, THAT I, WITH WINGS AS SWIFT
> AS MEDITATION OR THE THOUGHTS OF LOVE,
> MAY SWEEP TO MY REVENGE.

The story Claudius told was that old Hamlet was killed by a poisonous serpent as he slept in his orchard. But the truth, says the Ghost, is that "The serpent that did sting thy father's life/Now wears his crown."

Claudius is the murderer! "O my prophetic soul!" cries Hamlet. "My uncle!"

Yes, the Ghost explains: Claudius seduced Gertrude, then poured poison into King Hamlet's ears one afternoon, killing him before he could receive the sacrament of last rites, to remove any sin from his soul. He died "With all my imperfections on my head. /O horrible! O horrible! Most horrible!" But in demanding revenge on Claudius, the Ghost orders Hamlet to spare Gertrude:

> LEAVE HER TO HEAVEN,
> AND TO THOSE THORNS THAT IN HER BOSOM LODGE
> TO PRICK AND STING HER.

The Ghost returns to the underworld with the parting command: "Remember me," (although it is not likely that Hamlet will forget him.)

"Remember thee!" sobs Hamlet. He promises to "wipe away" from his memory

> ALL TRIVIAL FOND RECORDS,
> ALL SAWS OF BOOKS, ALL FORMS, ALL PRESSURES PAST,
> THAT YOUTH AND OBSERVATION COPIED THERE,
> AND THY COMMANDMENT ALL ALONE SHALL LIVE
> WITHIN THE BOOK AND VOLUME OF MY BRAIN,
> UNMIXED WITH BASER MATTER.

Horatio and Marcellus find Hamlet hysterical, not making much sense. He does not reveal what the Ghost has told him, ordering them: "Never make known what you have seen tonight." He insists that they swear by his sword. After they take the oath, the Ghost, under the earth, continues to cry out three times: "Swear."

Hamlet stipulates that they must never even hint that they know why he is behaving strangely, because in the future he may, he says, adopt an "antic disposition" for his own reasons. The two men accept all his conditions. As they part company Hamlet laments:

> THE TIME IS OUT OF JOINT. O CURSED SPITE,
> THAT EVER I WAS BORN TO SET IT RIGHT!

ANALYSIS

The Ghost's words imply that it is being temporarily punished in purgatory, not eternally in hell. But many commentators have questioned this, for good reason. Christianity condemns revenge as a grave sin. And, as we will see later, Hamlet himself thinks that true revenge would mean killing Claudius while he is guilty of some mortal sin, sending him to hell forever.

Hamlet at first accepts revenge eagerly and uncritically as his duty. He promises that the Ghost's command will exist "all alone" in his mind and memory. But of course that would mean a serious loss of proportion, sacrificing everything he has ever learned in favor of one obsessive purpose. He is incapable of being so imbalanced, and it is to his credit that this is so. By the end of the scene the supposed duty of revenge has already become an unbearable burden to him.

ACT II, SCENE 1

OVERVIEW

Polonius is sending his servant Reynaldo (who appears only in this scene and is not heard of again) to take notes and money to Laertes in Paris. He also wants Reynaldo to do some spying. He suggests that one way to elicit gossip about Laertes might be to lay "slight sullies" on him—to speak of his minor vices, such as gambling, drinking, swearing, or even "drabbing" (going to prostitutes). Reynaldo is shocked, saying, "My lord, that would dishonor him!" But Polonius thinks it will not, if done tactfully. As he often does, he becomes so tangled in his own words that he forgets what he was about to say.

After Reynaldo leaves, Ophelia rushes into the room, frightened. She explains that Hamlet is behaving very oddly, bursting into her chamber unannounced and staring wordlessly at her, then, with a long sigh, walking backward out the way he came. It is apparent that some time has passed, allowing for Hamlet to set his strategy in motion.

Polonius decides that Hamlet has gone mad out of love after Ophelia rejected him. He admits that he misjudged Hamlet when he warned Ophelia against him. But he feels he must tell the king about this.

ANALYSIS

Polonius is revealed as an inveterate spy who respects nobody's privacy, least of all his own daughter's. We are prepared by this scene for his snooping on Hamlet.

Ophelia reveals the weakness of her character, unable to stand up to her meddling father. We are not quite sure how to take her report of Hamlet's peculiar conduct. Is he pretending to be insane and trying to fool her, or is he testing her in the hope of being able to confide in her?

ACT II, SCENE 2

OVERVIEW

In this, the longest scene of the play (nine different characters appear in it), the mystery of the Ghost in the first act gradually becomes the broader mystery of human existence, as the characters try to figure one another out.

As the scene begins Claudius and Gertrude welcome two of Hamlet's old friends, Rosencrantz and Guildenstern, to court. They have been "brought up" with him, and Claudius hopes they can discover the cause of Hamlet's "transformation," since neither "the exterior nor the inward man" of Hamlet's character is what it was before.

As the friends depart, Polonius arrives with good news. First, the ambassadors to Norway have returned after a successful mission. More important, Polonius thinks he has found "the very cause of Hamlet's lunacy."

Voltemand and Cornelius report that the old king of Norway has been grieved to learn of his nephew Fortinbras's attempt to invade Denmark and has ordered Fortinbras to stop, paying him a handsome amount to take his army to attack Poland instead, passing peacefully through Denmark. Claudius is satisfied with this arrangement and thanks the two diplomats for their troubles.

For some reason Claudius is more concerned with his nephew's strange behavior than with any foreign danger, and Polonius begins his wordy explanation of his belief that Ophelia's rejection of Hamlet has driven him mad. (He lies about why she rejected him, saying that he merely told her that Hamlet's high social rank as a prince ruled him out as a potential husband for her; he says nothing about his real and more cynical reason: that he was suspicious of Hamlet's motives.) He reads aloud a love letter that he says Hamlet wrote to Ophelia, and adds that Hamlet has undergone a decline from depression at her rejection to his present madness. This, at least, is Polonius's theory.

Claudius, not quite persuaded, wants to test Polonius's theory further. Polonius notes that Hamlet often walks for hours "here in the lobby" and proposes that they watch him from behind an "arras" (curtain) when Hamlet thinks he is alone with Ophelia. Claudius agrees.

Just then Hamlet himself arrives, reading a book. Claudius and Gertrude leave Polonius with him.

Adopting his "antic disposition," Hamlet teases the old man with disguised witticisms about various subjects, including his daughter. Thinking Hamlet is truly mad, Polonius takes him seriously, but notices that he sometimes makes a strange kind of sense. He never suspects that Hamlet is making a fool of him.

This goes on until Polonius leaves and Rosencrantz and Guildenstern return. Hamlet is delighted to see his old friends and drops the pretense of madness.

They exchange mildly bawdy jokes until Hamlet asks them why fortune has sent them "to prison hither," because "Denmark's a prison."

After a little more conversation, Hamlet forces Rosencrantz and Guildenstern to admit that they have come to Denmark because the king and queen have sent for them. He then admits that he has been in poor

"WHAT A PIECE OF WORK IS MAN!"

spirits lately, though he says he can give no reason for it; he has lost his mirth, ceased taking exercise, and suffered a general disillusionment with man and the whole world. Man, who is "the beauty of the world, the paragon of animals," now seems to him "the quintessence of dust."

Rosencrantz tries to cheer Hamlet up by telling him that his favorite company of actors is coming to the court; Rosencrantz and Guildenstern have met them on the way. Hamlet is elated when the actors, also old friends of his, arrive at court. Polonius now reenters to announce what Hamlet already knows: that the actors are coming. Hamlet resumes baiting him about his daughter.

Hamlet greets the actors with real warmth, asking their star to recite one of Hamlet's favorite speeches, about the Trojan War, the slaughter of King Priam, and the grief of Queen Hecuba. The actor does so, breaking into tears as he delivers it.

Polonius is disgusted by this display of emotion, but Hamlet is moved and impressed. He orders Polonius to see that the actors are well taken care of. There will be a play at court tomorrow night.

Then he takes the leading actor aside and asks if the company can perform *The Murder of Gonzago*. The actor says yes. Hamlet then tells him that he will write a speech to be inserted into the play.

When he is alone Hamlet delivers by far the longest of his soliloquies, beginning "O what a rogue and peasant slave am I!" Most of it is violent self-reproach for his failure to keep the Ghost's command by killing Claudius.

Yet in the last few lines it takes a sudden turn. Hamlet—illogically, it seems—supposes that "the spirit that I have seen may be the devil" assuming his father's "shape" in order to "damn me" by provoking him to kill Claudius without justification. But the play to be presented tomorrow night will solve any mystery: If Claudius is guilty, his expression will show it when he sees his (alleged) crime reenacted on the stage. Hamlet ends the long speech with the cry

> THE PLAY'S THE THING
> WHEREIN I'LL CATCH THE CONSCIENCE OF THE KING!

ANALYSIS

This episodic scene seems to cover a long time; With the scene before it, which indicates that Laertes has been in Paris for a while, it gives us the impression that months have elapsed. Likewise the return of the two ambassadors from Norway implies some passage of time. Shakespeare manipulates our sense of time with admirable subtlety.

This is quite a change of pace from the first act, which covered less than two days! The dramatic fury of the early scenes is dissipated by this leisurely unfolding of events. Polonius's fussy wordiness as he relates his opinions increases our feeling that time is now passing slowly. As Hamlet baits him, as Rosencrantz and Guildenstern try to help the king and queen find the cause of Hamlet's odd behavior, as the actors come to Elsinore and prepare for the play, we nearly forget about the Ghost and the murder of Hamlet's father.

Then suddenly Hamlet's final soliloquy reminds us. He savagely upbraids (scolds) himself for his delay in killing Claudius, contrasting his own lack of emotion over his father's murder with the artificial passion of the actor over the grief of Hecuba.

Hamlet says he is "prompted to my revenge by heaven and hell" (words that invite reflection), but then says—for the first time, without any advance notice, at the very end of the scene—that "the spirit that I have seen may be the devil," impersonating his father's spirit.

This is a stunning development. After listening to the Ghost, Hamlet had assured Horatio and Marcellus that it was "an honest ghost." Now, some time later, he suggests the very opposite. And he has decided to use the device of a play, re-creating the alleged crime in front of Claudius, to test the Ghost's word.

Why has he come to doubt what he had been so sure of? How has he come to doubt the very duty of revenge that he promised he would "sweep" to when he told the Ghost he would keep its command "all alone" in his memory?

ACT III, SCENE 1

OVERVIEW

As Hamlet lays a trap for Claudius, Claudius and Polonius lay one for Hamlet.

Claudius questions Rosencrantz and Guildenstern about what they have managed to learn from Hamlet of the reason for his "transformation." They can report little except frustration; he received them "most like a gentleman," but volunteered no helpful information, except that he was adopting "a crafty madness."

But Claudius is pleased to learn that Hamlet's spirits are so good that he plans to stage a play for the court this very night, inviting the king to attend. Claudius, suspecting nothing beyond innocent amusement, agrees to come.

Meanwhile he and Polonius will hide behind a curtain to observe Hamlet with Ophelia. Polonius tells his daughter to read a religious book

"TO BE OR NOT TO BE: THAT IS THE QUESTION"

to create an impression of piety. He remarks regretfully on the hypocrisy of feigning religious appearances, and Claudius says, in an aside to the audience, that Polonius's remark stings his own bad conscience.

This is our first hint of what Hamlet will learn of the king's guilt. Claudius, by his own admission, is hiding something.

Claudius and Polonius conceal themselves as Gertrude, Rosencrantz, and Guildenstern depart and Hamlet comes in alone, delivering his most famous soliloquy: "To be or not to be." He compares death to a sleep in which we don't know whether we will dream, and to an "undiscovered country from whose bourn [boundary] no traveler returns." He is thinking of suicide, if death means an end of "the thousand natural shocks that flesh is heir to." But what if something worse follows after death? "Ay, there's the rub." This is why we finally decide to endure life after all: "Thus conscience does make cowards of us all." And in the end we may change all our great plans and do nothing.

Then he sees Ophelia and asks her prayers for "all my sins." She tells him that she wants to return the gifts—"remembrances"—he has given her. The word seems to ignite his fury; we recall his bitter memories of his mother ("Must I remember?") and his fervent vow to "remember" the Ghost.

Hamlet denies having given Ophelia anything and flies into a rage that she cannot comprehend. "Get thee to a nunnery," he tells her; "why wouldst thou be a breeder of sinners?" He is no worse than most men, he says, "yet it were better my mother had not borne me."

HAMLET, PLAYED BY KENNETH BRANAGH, AND OPHELIA, PLAYED BY KATE WINSLET, STARRED IN DIRECTOR BRANAGH'S 1996 PRODUCTION.

Suddenly suspicious he asks where her father is. Her lie—"at home"—only makes his anger more violent. He rails against her, her father, all women, and marriage, then leaves her by herself. The distraught Ophelia is now certain that he is insane.

Claudius and Polonius emerge from behind the curtain. The king now thinks Hamlet's passion has nothing to do with rejected love; he knows the prince is sane. Polonius offers his usual advice: to eavesdrop. After the play he will hide and listen to what Gertrude says to her son. If her scolding fails to correct him, he can be sent to England or put into confinement. Claudius agrees.

ANALYSIS

Now we are being prepared for the climactic confirmation of Claudius's guilt in the play scene. But there is no real mystery about it. Shakespeare tips us off by having Claudius reveal his bad conscience in a brief aside about his hypocrisy. Hamlet may be unsure of his uncle's guilt, but we are not.

Hamlet enters, deep in thought about whether it is nobler to suffer the outrages of fortune or to fight back. Is death really the end? It is the "undiscovered country" no traveler returns from—unless, of course, the problematic Ghost is such a traveler. But we cannot know, so we resign ourselves to the many evils we know in this life, made "cowards" by conscience and giving up on courageous action.

Noticing Ophelia, Hamlet breaks off thinking and questions her, not knowing that her father and Claudius are watching but nonetheless deeply suspicious of her. He turns on her all the anger that he has stored up against his mother; in his mind, all men are sinners and all women are seductresses.

Hearing Hamlet's explosion against women and marriage, Claudius realizes that whatever is preoccupying Hamlet, he is neither lovesick nor crazy; something must be done about him.

OVERVIEW

The fateful night commences. The play, *The Murder of Gonzago*, is about to begin. Hamlet advises the actors on how to deliver their lines, stressing the need for natural-seeming moderation and warning against overacting (but also against being "too tame"). He also urges that the clowns not be allowed to improvise or to add lines not in the script. Passion must be kept under control.

Now Hamlet turns to his friend Horatio, praising him with deep warmth for his self-control, his superiority to the whims and vicissitudes of fortune, for not being "passion's slave." The fiery, volatile Hamlet recognizes that Horatio, steadily calm and rational, is, temperamentally, both his opposite and his superior. In short Horatio is the soul of reason.

Returning to the immediate situation, Hamlet tells Horatio that the play will reenact what the Ghost has confided to him about King Hamlet's murder. If Claudius's reaction to the scene fails to expose "his occulted guilt," then "it is a damned ghost that we have seen." Horatio agrees to observe Claudius closely.

They join the courtiers to watch the play. Forgetting all his own counsel against being controlled by passion, Hamlet baits everyone with sarcasm—Polonius, Claudius, Gertrude, and, most obscenely, Ophelia.

The play begins with a dumb show, or wordless pantomime, showing the murder. Hamlet, vexed, expresses irritation. The actors perform the story again, this time aloud, according to the script Hamlet has written himself. It is designed to implicate Gertrude, whom Hamlet suspects of complicity in the murder, but Gertrude fails to perceive this.

He continues to comment freely as the play proceeds, the actor playing the queen falsely promises to be faithful to her husband's memory if he dies. Hamlet is sure this "wormwood" must be galling to her, but Gertrude still fails to see any parallel to herself. Hamlet asks how she likes the play; she answers obtusely, "The lady doth protest too much, methinks."

Claudius, however, has begun to suspect something. He asks Hamlet if there is any "offense" in the story. Not at all, Hamlet says merrily: "Your majesty, and we that have free souls, it touches us not."

At last the actor playing the murderer makes his entrance with the poison he intends to use to kill the actor playing the king. Hamlet identifies him as "Lucianus, nephew to the king." As he pours the poison into his victim's ear, Hamlet cries: "He poisons him i'th' garden for his estate. . . . You shall see anon how the murderer gets the love of Gonzago's wife."

These impulsive comments confuse the courtiers, who think Hamlet, a nephew, is somehow threatening to kill Claudius. But Claudius himself grasps the point: Hamlet knows about his crime!

Claudius rises, calling for light. The play breaks up. The courtiers depart with the king, leaving Hamlet and Horatio by themselves.

Hamlet is elated, triumphant. He has learned what he wanted to know. His hated uncle is guilty! "O good Horatio, I'll take the Ghost's word for a thousand pound. Didst perceive? . . . Upon the talk of the poisoning?"

Yes, Horatio has seen it all, but is more subdued. He realizes that Hamlet, carried away by emotion, has misplayed his opportunity. The apparent victory will bring new dangers.

Rosencrantz and Guildenstern enter. Hamlet calls for recorder music to celebrate. His old friends tell him that Claudius and Gertrude are very upset with him, and that the queen wants to see him in her chamber. Hamlet replies with gloating sarcasm; he now regards these old friends as contemptible enemies.

They are still baffled by his behavior. He says the reason for the way he is acting is that he lacks "advancement." But, says Rosencrantz, the king himself has already announced that Hamlet will succeed him! Hamlet replies by partially citing the old proverb "While the grass grows, the horse starves": He does not intend to wait for Claudius to die.

He challenges Guildenstern to play the recorder; when Guildenstern replies that he cannot, Hamlet unloads further sarcasm on him: "You would play upon me. . . . [D]o you think that I am easier to be played on than a pipe?"

Polonius arrives and tells Hamlet again that Gertrude wants to speak with him at once. Hamlet teases the old man again, but agrees to see her.

Left alone Hamlet reflects that this is the witching hour, and he feels ready to "drink hot blood": He must not yield to "the soul of Nero" and kill his own mother. He is tempted to kill her, not Claudius.

ANALYSIS

In two speeches, first to the actors and then to Horatio, Hamlet discourses on the virtue of keeping passion under control. But throughout the scene his own passions get the better of him. He taunts everyone at court and all but ruins the play he has so carefully planned.

He cannot shake his baseless suspicion that his mother has helped Claudius murder his father. He writes this into the script of *The Murder of Gonzago* to test her reaction, then fails to notice when she seems to be quite innocent.

That script repeats the theme of passion:

> WHAT TO OURSELVES IN PASSION WE PROPOSE,
> THE PASSION ENDING, DOTH THE PURPOSE LOSE.

> OUR WILLS AND FATES DO SO CONTRARY RUN
> THAT OUR DEVICES STILL ARE OVERTHROWN;
> OUR THOUGHTS ARE OURS, THEIR ENDS NONE
> OF OUR OWN.

These passages might serve as good comments on Hamlet himself.

Hamlet thinks the play device has succeeded when Claudius reveals his guilt to Hamlet and Horatio, but the other courtiers, disturbed by Hamlet's "antic" behavior, never perceive that Claudius is guilty. They just think their belief is confirmed that the prince is simply deranged or irresponsible.

After Claudius interrupts the play, Hamlet rashly assumes that he has won the battle of wits. Horatio, always more sober, knows better.

The entrance of Rosencrantz and Guildenstern proves that Horatio is correct. They give no indication of realizing the true meaning of Claudius's behavior; it is Hamlet's behavior that concerns and baffles them. Likewise Polonius sees only that Hamlet is still acting wildly.

In his soliloquy ending the scene, Hamlet reveals that his passion is still dangerously out of his own control: He fears he may kill not his uncle, but his mother.

ACT III, SCENE 3

OVERVIEW

Claudius orders Rosencrantz and Guildenstern to prepare to escort Hamlet to England. He is too dangerous to be permitted to stay in Denmark. They agree, of course, having missed the whole point of Claudius's own explosion at the play.

Polonius, wordy as always, tells Claudius that Hamlet is on his way to Gertrude's chamber, where Polonius himself will be hiding to overhear whatever is said.

Now Claudius is alone, and he delivers his own long soliloquy. He is sick with guilt at his crime, the crime of Cain in the Bible, "a brother's murder." He is torn. He wants to repent, but he cannot bear to give up the fruits of his crime: "my crown, mine own ambition, and my queen." In this world, he reflects, a man can have it both ways, but not in heaven. He falls to his knees, trying to pray.

As he kneels Hamlet comes by and, seeing his chance for revenge, draws his sword: "Now might I do it pat, now he is praying." But he immediately reasons that if he kills Claudius at prayer, the king may go straight to heaven! "Why, this is hire and salary, not revenge." After all Claudius killed Hamlet's father "grossly," "With all his crimes broad-blown, as flush as May," so why should Hamlet kill him in "the purging of his soul/When he is fit and season'd for his passage?"

A 1994 PRODUCTION AT THE OPEN AIR THEATER IN LONDON FEATURED DAMIEN LEWIS AS HAMLET AND PAUL FREEMAN AS KING CLAUDIUS.

Sheathing his sword Hamlet decides to delay his revenge until he can catch his uncle committing a sin, perhaps "in the incestuous pleasure of his bed," so that "his soul may be as damn'd and black as hell, Whereto it goes."

But as soon as Hamlet has gone, Claudius rises. He has been unable to pray sincerely. He realizes that he has chosen damnation after all.

ANALYSIS

This scene makes it clear that Hamlet knows that his father's Ghost has come from hell, not purgatory. He has died without the sacraments in the midst of his "crimes"—"foul crimes," as he called them.

The eighteenth-century English literary critic Samuel Johnson called Hamlet's soliloquy "too horrible to be read or uttered," because the prince is not content with mere justice—blood for blood—but actually seeks to damn his enemy's soul, which is itself a damnable sin.

Fierce as this may sound, Hamlet still seems less angry at his uncle than at his mother.

ACT III, SCENE 4

OVERVIEW

In Gertrude's chamber Polonius urges the queen to scold her son severely for his "pranks"; the old man still cannot comprehend the real gravity of the situation. He hides behind a hanging tapestry as Hamlet approaches.

When Hamlet arrives Gertrude accuses him: "Hamlet, thou hast thy father much offended"—meaning Claudius. He retorts, "Mother, you have my father much offended"—meaning that she has murdered his real father. Seeing his fury, she thinks he is about to kill her and calls for help. Polonius calls for help, too. Hearing the voice Hamlet stabs through the tapestry, thinking it is Claudius. He lifts the tapestry and finds that he has killed Polonius.

When Gertrude calls this “a rash and bloody deed,” Hamlet retorts: “A bloody deed! Almost as bad, good mother,/As kill a king and marry with his brother.” She gasps, “As kill a king?” Suddenly he realizes that she is innocent of his father’s murder. He hurls abuse at Polonius’s corpse: “Thou wretched, rash, intruding fool, farewell./I took thee for thy better.”

ANALYSIS

Hamlet here turns the tables on himself. He had first had the inspired thought of exposing his uncle’s guilt by staging a play reenacting the murder of his father; but he partly wasted the opportunity by letting his passions get the better of him (despite his own wise words to both the actors and Horatio about self-control) so that everyone at court except Claudius (and Horatio) missed the point, thinking Hamlet was insanely threatening the king.

Now, in his anger at Gertrude’s sins, his passions betray him again: He draws his sword on her, frightening her so badly that she calls for help. When Polonius, hiding behind the tapestry, joins her cry, Hamlet impulsively stabs him, mistaking him for Claudius. This killing puts him in his enemy’s power. He has lost the advantage and initiative he enjoyed at the beginning of the evening. And he has also, as we see later, made another deadly enemy: Polonius’s son, Laertes.

In his cooler moments, Hamlet has never really wanted to kill Claudius, much as he hates him. Now he turns his rage on his mother for her sins of lust. His fury at her is so violent that the Ghost appears to him (but remains invisible to Gertrude) to remind him that he is supposed to kill Claudius, not to vent his passion at his mother.

But it is too late. Hamlet is now being sent to England by Claudius’s order. He has wasted his chance to put Claudius at his mercy, and now his own life is in grave danger.

ACT IV, SCENE 1

OVERVIEW

Claudius finds Gertrude in great agitation, tearful and sighing. He asks her what has upset her, but she, now suspicious of her husband, gives him a shaded account of events. Hamlet, in a mad moment, has mistaken Polonius for a rat and stabbed him to death. Thinking first of himself, as always, Claudius realizes that had he been there, he would have met the same fate. He calls Rosencrantz and Guildenstern and orders them to bring Hamlet and Polonius's body.

ANALYSIS

Gertrude is now unsure what to think, but she instinctively tries to protect her son from her self-centered husband. Claudius's suave charm cannot conceal his essential cynicism.

ACT IV, SCENE 2

OVERVIEW

Hamlet teases Rosencrantz and Guildenstern about where he has stowed the body, turning it into a game of hide-and-seek. He also taunts them about their sycophantic obedience to the king.

ANALYSIS

Hamlet despises his old schoolfellows for their lack of character. Unlike his only real friend, Horatio, they are amoral puppets of chance, willing to do whatever they are told.

ACT IV, SCENE 3

OVERVIEW

Rosencrantz and Guildenstern bring Hamlet to the king under guard. Ever the smooth hypocrite, Claudius feigns love for his nephew. But of course Hamlet is undeceived and replies, as always, with his own insolent wit. When Claudius tells Hamlet he must go to England—for his own good, of course—Hamlet fully realizes that he is going to be murdered there. After he is escorted away, Claudius, in a soliloquy, expresses his eagerness for his nephew's death in England, for which he has already sealed a written order. (England, in the story, is a territory under Denmark's control.)

ANALYSIS

The enmity between Hamlet and Claudius is now all but open. Among the play's characters, only Rosencrantz and Guildenstern are still fooled, thinking that Claudius means well and that Hamlet is the sole troublemaker. Hamlet stings his uncle with some of his most piercing witticisms, such as when he explains how "a king may go a progress through the guts of a beggar."

ACT IV, SCENE 4

OVERVIEW

Fortinbras of Norway arrives on Danish soil with his army. He plans to invade Poland and gives assurances that he has no hostile or aggressive intentions toward Denmark.

In his final soliloquy, Hamlet, who is on his way to England when he meets this army, once again expresses shame that he has delayed his revenge so long. He feels shamed by the courage of the Norwegians, who are ready to shed their blood over a mere patch of Polish territory, a plot of ground too small to bury the men who will die fighting for it.

ANALYSIS

This short scene includes a soliloquy on revenge that tells us almost nothing beyond what we already knew. Hamlet, now under the control of others, has lost the ability to act on his intentions, making the soliloquy futile. There is some evidence that Shakespeare cut the speech in his final revision of the play.

OVERVIEW

The content clues in this scene indicate the second long passage of time in the events of the play. Ophelia has gone mad. Her father is dead, killed by Hamlet, who has violently rejected her. Meanwhile her brother, Laertes, has been gone for months. She is friendless. She sings bits of old songs without making much sense, and she hands out flowers to everyone around her.

Gertrude is now guilt-stricken about her marriage. The sight of the raving Ophelia adds to her unease. Claudius comments on the multiplicity of sorrows.

Just when it seems as if things could hardly get worse, Laertes arrives home from France, leading a riotous mob that wants to make him their new king. He is enraged to hear of Polonius's death and demands to know how it happened so he can take revenge.

Claudius handles Laertes deftly, promising to give him justice and affirming his own innocence without saying anything to frighten Gertrude. Poor Ophelia enters, singing mad ballads, and Laertes's wrath is redoubled. All is going well for Claudius, it seems.

ANALYSIS

Claudius's cool hypocrisy reaches its nadir, or lowest point, when he tells his attendants to let the furious Laertes go. The king is safe from any harm, he says, because God protects kings from treason.

Laertes has no qualms about revenge:

> TO HELL, ALLEGIANCE! VOWS TO THE BLACKEST DEVIL!
> CONSCIENCE AND GRACE TO THE PROFOUNDEST PIT!
> I DARE DAMNATION! TO THIS POINT I STAND,
> THAT BOTH THE WORLDS I GIVE TO NEGLIGENCE,
> LET COME WHAT COMES; ONLY I'LL BE REVENGED
> MOST THOROUGHLY FOR MY FATHER.

He could hardly be more explicit than that. Unlike Hamlet, who says he is prompted to his revenge "by heaven and hell," Laertes takes a purely hellish view of it.

Revenge is satanic. This is the last word on the Ghost's fierce commandment to Hamlet.

OVERVIEW

Horatio meets two sailors who bring him letters from Hamlet, one for him and some for the king and queen. Horatio reads that the sailors are pirates who overtook the ship that was taking Hamlet to England, captured him, and treated him well, knowing who he was. Now he owes them a good turn.

Hamlet says he will also tell Horatio other news when he sees him, particularly news about Rosencrantz and Guildenstern. Horatio tells the men to take him to Hamlet.

ANALYSIS

This brief scene serves to tell us that Hamlet has never arrived in England and has come home. As always he relies on Horatio.

ACT IV, SCENE 7

OVERVIEW

Having convinced Laertes that Hamlet was responsible for Polonius's death, Claudius is surprised to find out from Hamlet's letter that he is alive and back in Denmark. Claudius and Laertes plot Hamlet's death. They will use the king's favorite weapon: poison. They will stage a fencing match, and Laertes's rapier will have its tip treated with a venomous poison he has bought from a mountebank, or quack doctor. Hamlet will be too trusting to suspect mischief. But in case that fails, Claudius has a backup plan: poisoned wine for Hamlet to drink.

As they conspire, Gertrude brings shocking news: Ophelia has drowned, apparently a suicide. Laertes's hunger for revenge is intensified by this new grief.

ANALYSIS

Emboldened by his successful crimes, Claudius is sure that his new plan to kill Hamlet is foolproof.

ACT V, SCENE 1

OVERVIEW

Two gravediggers, ignorant but no less sure of themselves for that, argue over the legalities of Ophelia's funeral. If she committed suicide, how can she be allowed a Christian burial? Somehow the coroner has ruled that she may. The two men agree that she is actually being allowed a regular funeral only because of her high social rank as a gentlewoman.

SIR JOHN MILLAIS'S 1852 OIL ON CANVAS ROMANTICALLY DEPICTS OPHELIA'S DROWNING.

It may be wrong, but this is the way this world works and they can do nothing about it.

Hamlet and Horatio arrive at the graveyard, and Hamlet is slightly shocked and amused to hear one of the men singing as he digs a grave. (Horatio does not tell Hamlet for whom the grave is being dug. Either this is an oversight on Shakespeare's part or he assumes that the audience will not notice.)

As the gravedigger tosses old skulls out of the ground, Hamlet playfully wonders whose they may be. A politician's? A courtier's? A lord's? A lawyer's?

Hamlet questions the man about his grim trade, and the gravedigger answers with earthy humor, offering the prince a skull that once belonged to Yorick, the king's jester. Hamlet is amazed. Taking the skull in his hand,

"A MINISTERING ANGEL SHALL MY SISTER BE"

he recalls that Yorick used to carry him on his back and kiss him when he was a small boy; now the memory disgusts him. He tells the skull to go to "my lady's chamber" and bid her apply her makeup an inch thick; she will end up looking just like this anyway.

Hamlet keeps meditating and joking in this morbid vein, with Horatio mildly protesting that he is overdoing it, until he notices Claudius, Gertrude, Laertes, and the courtiers coming for the funeral. He is stunned when he realizes whose body they are following: Ophelia's!

Gertrude gently throws flowers on the corpse: "Sweets to the sweet." Laertes rages at the priest for denying Ophelia a full funeral service. The priest retorts that she would have been buried in unsanctified ground except that "great command"—meaning a special order from the king—had overruled the proper procedure.

Hamlet watches in horror as Laertes, wailing, leaps into the grave, hugs the corpse, and curses the man who caused her death. At this Hamlet steps forth and challenges Laertes, leaping into the grave to grapple with him. "The devil take thy soul!" Laertes cries. "Thou pray'st not well," quips Hamlet as Laertes tries to strangle him. Now everyone is yelling. Even Horatio tells Hamlet to calm down, saying, "Good my lord, be quiet!"

When peace is restored, Hamlet cannot understand Laertes's anger at him. Claudius counsels Laertes to be patient and follow their plan.

IN ZEFFIRELLI'S 1990 FILM PRODUCTION, MEL GIBSON AS HAMLET ADDRESSES YORICK'S SKULL.

ANALYSIS

This scene gives us one of the most emblematic moments in Western literature: Hamlet holding Yorick's skull. He confronts the mystery of death on the very day he himself is to die. One might say that this is Shakespeare's most Shakespearean scene.

Yet again we see Hamlet's versatile wit in action as his mind plays on the many facets of dying and decay. He ranges from the law to ancient history to "my lady's chamber," generalizing philosophically without suspecting how imminent his own end is. He can meditate abstractly on death as the real men around him are scheming to kill him without his knowing it.

And, as usual, the sturdy Horatio seems to have more presence of mind. His head is never lost in the clouds. He is not at all puzzled as to why Laertes hates Hamlet. The other characters live in the immediate moment, coping with their various practical problems. Hamlet acts as if he is going to live forever in the leisure of his own incomparable mind.

ACT V, SCENE 2

OVERVIEW

THERE'S A DIVINITY THAT SHAPES OUR ENDS, ROUGH-HEW THEM HOW WE WILL.

With this famous comment as prologue, Hamlet tells Horatio how he discovered, and defeated, Claudius's plan to have him murdered in England.

Unable to sleep on the ship one night, he opened the sealed letters and found the order that he should be beheaded as soon as he arrived. So, using his own familiarity with diplomatic language, he forged and substituted his own order: that Rosencrantz and Guildenstern should be put to death without even being allowed time for final confession.

Horatio is quietly shocked. He asks how this forged order was sealed. "Why, even in that was heaven ordinant," explains Hamlet. "I had my father's signet in my purse." This ring, for certifying official documents, enabled him to doom Rosencrantz and Guildenstern without the sacraments—just as his father had been doomed by Claudius.

When Horatio indicates quiet disapproval, Hamlet insists that "they are not near my conscience." After all, they asked for trouble by interfering in the battle of "mighty opposites," Hamlet and the king. Hamlet insists that it will also be "perfect conscience" to kill Claudius for his crimes and sins. And he adds that he now understands Laertes's outrage, since his cause—avenging a slain father—mirrors Hamlet's own.

At this point the courtier Osric approaches, making arrangements for the fencing match. Hamlet's mockery of Osric's precious manners goes over his head.

It is now time for the match. Hamlet has misgivings, but he dismisses Horatio's advice to heed them. He feels ready for anything, even death. He apologizes to Laertes, blaming his "madness" for Polonius's death, and Laertes pretends to accept this.

The match begins with Hamlet scoring two quick points. Gertrude, as a toast, drinks from the poisoned cup despite Claudius's attempt to stop her: "Gertrude, do not drink." When Hamlet fails to score a third point, Laertes cheats during the pause and slightly wounds him with the rapier's poisoned tip. Hamlet, enraged, forces an exchange of rapiers and wounds Laertes. Gertrude falls. In a flash Claudius's plot has unraveled: Hamlet, Laertes, and Gertrude are all about to die.

Gertrude cries that she has been poisoned. Hamlet, seeing "villainy," furiously calls for the door to be locked. Laertes realizes that all is lost and confesses: He and Hamlet are both poisoned. Gertrude is poisoned, too, and "the king's to blame."

Hamlet stabs Claudius with the poisoned rapier and pours some of the poisoned wine down his throat. As Claudius dies, Laertes begs Hamlet to "exchange forgiveness with me." Hamlet pardons him and says farewell to his dead mother.

Time has run out. Hamlet urgently orders Horatio to tell the whole story so that the world will understand his actions, sparing him "a wounded name"; Horatio wants to drink the poisoned wine, too, but Hamlet's dying anguish dissuades him.

Now Fortinbras arrives, freshly victorious from Poland. Hamlet predicts that he will be chosen Denmark's new king and endorses this result: "He has my dying voice." He breaks off in mid-sentence with his final words: "The rest is silence."

Not only Fortinbras but the English ambassador also arrives to tell Claudius that his order has been executed: Rosencrantz and Guildenstern are dead. The grieving Horatio tells both men that he will explain everything. Fortinbras orders that Hamlet, in death, be honored as a great warrior.

ANALYSIS

Recounting his adventures to Horatio, Hamlet sees no irony in his having done to Rosencrantz and Guildenstern what Claudius did to old King Hamlet: consigned them to death without the sacraments. With no sense of irony he says it was divine providence that enabled him to do this. It seems not to occur to him that both men were innocent. As far as they knew, they were simply serving their lawful monarch. They knew nothing of the murder that made him king or of his sealed orders for Hamlet's death.

Yet after this Hamlet appears to be at his happiest and most magnanimous. He sees Laertes's point of view and tries to make peace with him. He speaks to Claudius and Gertrude without spite or sarcasm. He is resigned to death, if that is God's will. This is a Hamlet we have hardly seen before.

And so Shakespeare's richest creation goes to his doom. His final thoughts are for the fate of Denmark and for his own reputation. Shakespeare never made a more awesome character; only in *King Lear* would he imagine a more awesome world.

LIST OF MAJOR CHARACTERS

Hamlet, prince of Denmark

Claudius, king of Denmark, uncle of Hamlet

Ghost of King Hamlet, father of the prince

Gertrude, queen of Denmark, Hamlet's widowed mother, now married to Claudius

Polonius, counselor of Claudius

Laertes, son of Polonius

Ophelia, daughter of Polonius

Horatio, friend and fellow student of Hamlet

ANALYSIS OF MAJOR CHARACTERS

HAMLET

It has often been truly observed that Shakespeare has put more of his own inexhaustible genius into Hamlet—poetic, superbly eloquent, witty, speculative, generous, cunning, imaginatively fertile, emotionally unpredictable—than into any other character; he is the only character we can imagine writing Shakespeare's plays. He towers above even the Bard's other greatest creations—the characters of Falstaff, Iago, and Cleopatra—though his rich personality also includes parts of each of them.

Beyond any doubt Hamlet is the most debated figure in world literature. Countless books have been written about him, as if he were a real historical figure. By some accounts more books have been written about him than about any real men in history, except Jesus, Napoleon, Lincoln, and Hitler. Commentators have discussed at great length questions such as whether his madness is real or merely pretended, and why he delays his revenge so long. In the words of one critic, Shakespeare's characters seem so real because they are "as opaque as life's"; we can never quite have the last word about them. There is always more to be said. And this is especially true of Hamlet.

The fact is illustrated by the variety of interpretations he has received in the theater. Every actor wants to play this towering role, but no two actors play him in quite the same way, as can be seen by comparing the filmed versions of Laurence Olivier, Richard Burton, Nicol Williamson, Derek Jacobi, Mel Gibson, Kenneth Branagh, and Ethan Hawke. All of them have their virtues, but none is definitive. Some of them seem almost opposite: Olivier's fiery, athletic, heroic Hamlet could hardly be more unlike Branagh's light and whimsical prince, but who is to say that either is wrong? The character has room for all these readings, and many more.

Hamlet's wit is manifest from the first line he speaks: "A little more than kin, and less than kind." This at once sets him apart from the rest of the Danish court. Like most of Shakespeare's villains, oddly, he rejects the festivity of the society around him, but we soon learn that he is right to do so. Denmark is prematurely celebrating the arrival of a new king after the death of its old one. Its widowed queen has entered into a swift and scandalous marriage (an incestuous one, in fact) with her late husband's brother. The court's tolerance of this irregular union is a measure of its amorality.

Hamlet despises his uncle and makes no effort to hide his contempt, even before he learns of his father's murder. He is sick with horror at his mother's behavior and wishes he could die. He longs to return to school at Wittenberg, where he can savor the quiet joys of a contemplative life, away from the corruption and strife of politics.

SIR LAURENCE OLIVIER WON AN OSCAR AND A GOLDEN GLOBE FOR HIS PORTRAYAL OF HAMLET IN THE 1948 BRITISH FILM PRODUCTION.

With his social inferiors, especially his fellow scholar Horatio, Hamlet is unfailingly gracious until he has reason to suspect them of betraying him to Claudius. He is shrewd enough to see through the scheming Polonius at once; his pure love for Ophelia is spoiled when she rejects him in obedience to her father and helps Polonius and Claudius spy on him. He warmly welcomes his old friends Rosencrantz and Guildenstern to court until he realizes that they, too, are working for his enemies.

"'TIS NOW THE VERY WITCHING TIME OF NIGHT"

The arrival of the actors at Elsinore also delights him. They, at least, are his friends, and he sees how they can help him defeat the forces arrayed against him. For a few minutes he loses himself in a discussion of the art of acting, the essence of which, he explains, is "to hold, as't were, the mirror up to nature" by avoiding excesses of passion, clowning, and calling attention to oneself (good advice, which he himself forgets before the play has even begun). Hamlet's essential sweetness becomes clearest when he is alone with Horatio, before the play in Act III, before Ophelia's funeral in Act V, and again before the fatal fencing match with Laertes in the same act. Horatio is the only character with whom he is fully rational. (It is no accident that the name *Horatio* includes the Latin word for reason, *ratio*.)

Hamlet cherishes the memory of his dead father, whom he virtually worships: Compared to Claudius, he says, old Hamlet was Hyperion, the sun god, compared to a satyr, a lecherous figure of myth. He wonders how his mother could have preferred the miserable Claudius to such a man, whom he also likens to Hercules, Mercury, and Mars. (Significantly, the old man had "an eye like Mars"—the Roman god of war—"to threaten and command.") But all this excessive praise of his father makes him sound more like a forbidding figure of awe than a loving, or lovable, husband and parent.

For most of the play Hamlet seems to hate Polonius even more than he hates Claudius, though the meddling old man is more foolish and annoying than wicked. It is true that Claudius has murdered his father and seduced and corrupted his mother; Polonius has merely deprived him of Ophelia (for surely he realizes, when she refuses to see him and sends back his letters, that this must be at her father's command).

Although Hamlet is extremely intelligent, he shows a curious blindness in one key respect. He idealizes his father and can see no redeeming virtues in Claudius. In fact he can hardly bring himself to admit that Claudius is human. In this he is seriously unrealistic. Time and again Hamlet attributes to his father the qualities of pagan gods and heroes (but never, significantly, the Christian saints), whereas he persistently disparages his uncle as a satyr, a slave, a villain, a rat, a toad ("paddock"), a bat, a "cutpurse," a "bloat king," a tomcat ("gib"), and much more. The Ghost uses similar invectives, calling Claudius a "wretch" and "garbage" and himself "a radiant angel"—after admitting that he is consigned to suffer in fire for his own "foul crimes"!

Hamlet's self-contradictions reach their lowest point when he actually fears that his (apparently praying) uncle may be repenting and going to heaven, while his father is being punished for dying "with all his crimes broad blown as flush as May." This is why Samuel Johnson and other Christian readers have been appalled by the speech beginning "Now might I do it pat."

Hamlet's unreasoning hatred of Claudius spills over into hostility toward anyone he perceives as an agent of the king, such as Polonius (and, by extension, Ophelia). He never stops to ask himself why people who know nothing of the Ghost and the murder should not try to serve and

protect their king. To the court it appears that Hamlet is making insanely wild and treasonous threats against a lawful monarch. Rosencrantz and Guildenstern argue reasonably that it is "most holy and religious fear" to defend the king (and Denmark as a whole) against such threats. For this reason they agree to escort Hamlet to England. They know neither of the murder of the old king nor of Claudius's secret order for Hamlet's murder; yet Hamlet calls these innocent men "adders fanged" and sends them to their death with his own forged order, callously remarking that "They are not near my conscience."

Many critics who see all the play's events only from Hamlet's perspective and share his obsession with Claudius's guilt fail to see that Hamlet is incurring some guilt of his own; his remark about the merry gravedigger who sings as he works applies to Hamlet, too: "The hand of little employment hath the daintier sense." We see his coarsening when, having killed Polonius, he quips cruelly, "I'll lug the guts into the neighbor room." He is at first unable to grasp why Laertes hates him and also blames him for Ophelia's madness and death. He has been corrupted, and morally blinded, by the Ghost's demand for revenge. Horatio and Marcellus were right to warn him against following that sinister figure.

To see Hamlet as an innocent and righteous avenger is to miss the point of the tragedy. He becomes part of Denmark's rottenness and helps bring about its ruin. Claudius asks the furious Laertes,

IS'T WRIT IN YOUR REVENGE
THAT, SWOOPSTAKE, YOU WILL DRAW BOTH FRIEND AND FOE,
WINNER AND LOSER?

"None but his enemies," Laertes replies. But Claudius speaks more wisely than he knows: Revenge by its nature is indiscriminate; it sweeps the innocent and the guilty together.

"ROSENCRANTZ AND GUILDENSTERN ARE DEAD"

Hamlet's revenge will finally claim not only Claudius, but Hamlet himself, Gertrude (whom the Ghost ordered Hamlet to spare), and several others. In the end the kingdom of Denmark itself falls in conquest to its old enemy, Norway. Can this be what the Ghost wanted when it made its first appearance in the story?

Maybe the play as a whole says to the Ghost, in effect, what Portia says to Shylock in *The Merchant of Venice*: "Thou shalt have justice—more than thou desirest." What is notably missing in the Denmark of *Hamlet* is mercy.

CLAUDIUS

The villain of *Hamlet*, the murderer of his own brother, is a brilliant, resourceful man, a worthy antagonist for his gifted nephew. Claudius is a smooth talker who knows how to use power and handle people deftly. He proves that he is both shrewd and courageous. He is quick to sense danger from Hamlet and ruthless in protecting himself from every threat to his rule over Denmark.

Claudius sincerely loves Hamlet's mother, a still-attractive woman who is his equal in intelligence. He has married her to gain the Danish throne, but he clearly values her for her human qualities, too. Though he is not afraid of a fight, he is prudent enough to avoid conflict whenever possible. He quickly pacifies the outraged Laertes and, with marvelous tact, draws him into a conspiracy to murder Hamlet.

Although Claudius is supposedly his brother's opposite, he is not. If we listen to Hamlet and the Ghost we are apt to mistake Claudius for a simple villain, when in fact he is anything but that. His conscience tortures him about the act he has committed, the crime of Cain, "a brother's murder." He could be the subject of his own separate tragedy, like *Macbeth*. In the end his evil choices cancel out all his good qualities, which his nephew mercilessly refuses to acknowledge (even as he counts on Claudius's conscience to give away his guilt during the play, as indeed it does).

Hamlet and his father have their own sins to answer for. Almost the first thing the Ghost says is that he is being fearfully punished for his sins, a fact that hardly registers with Hamlet, who continues to idealize him and contrast him with Claudius anyway. Both common sense and religion (not to mention his own personal experience) should have warned Hamlet against imagining that two brothers could be as diametrically opposed as he imagines them to be. Hate can breed wishful thinking as surely as love does. Hamlet *wants* his uncle to be as bad as possible.

Yet part of Claudius desperately wants to repent. After the play within the play we see him fall to his knees and try to pray. In his one long soliloquy (one that was deeply admired by Abraham Lincoln) he meditates as profoundly and passionately as Hamlet himself. What a terrible pity that these two men could not have been friends!

But Hamlet insists on idealizing his father and demonizing Claudius with equal unrealism. Far too many critics of the play have allowed themselves to be drawn into Hamlet's delusion that these brothers have nothing in common. From this it is a short step to justifying Hamlet's supposed duty of revenge and missing the point of the tragedy.

GHOST

The Ghost is the spirit of hate, war, and violence. It appears in armor, "warlike," shrinks from the morning light, and appears "guilty." The shrewd and spiritually alert Horatio, who tries to induce it to talk, fears the worst: He tries to dissuade Hamlet from following it and speaking to it alone.

Whether it is, as Hamlet says, "an honest ghost"—telling the literal truth about Claudius's murder of his brother—is beside the point. As Banquo says in *Macbeth*, hellish spirits may use even the truth to trick us into damning ourselves:

> OFTENTIMES, TO WIN US TO OUR HARM,
> THE INSTRUMENTS OF DARKNESS TELL US TRUTHS,
> WIN US WITH HONEST TRIFLES, TO BETRAY 'S
> IN DEEPEST CONSEQUENCE.

If the Ghost's real purpose is to win Hamlet to his harm, damnation, then the accurate report of the murder in the orchard can be seen as an "honest trifle," and Hamlet is wasting his time trying to prove by experiment (testing Claudius's reaction to the play within the play) whether it is true. Hamlet commits a non sequitur (uses faulty logic) when he reasons that if the Ghost has told the truth about the crime, his revenge will be justified; but at first viewing or reading, we are apt to be swept along with him by our own passions, confusing angry revenge with impartial justice.

The mystery of the Ghost is never resolved for us; it remains an enigma. Is it distressed by the deaths of Hamlet and Gertrude and by the devastation of the Danish kingdom, or is all this ruin the fulfillment of its ultimate diabolical plan? Shakespeare leaves these questions unanswered, "Thoughts beyond the reaches of our souls."

"FRAILTY, THY NAME IS WOMAN"

GERTRUDE

Hamlet's mother has usually been regarded as a weak, stupid, passive woman. She is not. Her mind, like her son's, is quick and concise, going straight to the heart of a question. She is nobody's fool. She wittily prods the long-winded Polonius to stop being so wordy and get to the point: "More matter with less art." He says, but does not know as she does, that "brevity is the soul of wit"—that is, "wit" in its old sense of intelligence and discernment, not just cleverness.

Though she is sinfully married to her brother-in-law and has weaknesses both for sexual indulgence and drink, she carries herself with dignity and has insight into other people. Her sympathy for Ophelia, who she hoped would marry her son, is especially touching. She is also aware that Hamlet's grief for his father's death is excessive and spiritually unhealthy, even dangerous.

For most of the play Hamlet wrongly believes that Gertrude helped Claudius kill his father, which is why he is tempted to kill her. This disastrous sin and crime is barely averted when Hamlet sees, at the moment of Polonius's death, that she is astonished at his suspicion; she is not even aware that Claudius is guilty of murdering her first husband. Hamlet still heaps abuse on her, but now it is merely for marrying Claudius; he has to drop the charge of murder that had weighed so heavily on his mind.

Gertrude tries to be loyal to both her son and her husband. The situation is painful and extremely confusing for her. Hamlet appears to be insane, killing Polonius and talking to a ghost that is invisible to her, but she wants to protect him as best she can from Claudius's wrath after the “bloody deed.” At any rate we do her serious wrong to dismiss her as the “dull and shallow woman” so many critics have accused her of being. She mediates between the warring men in her life with great skill, and we have to try to imagine the tangled situation as it must appear to her. Naturally she would prefer to believe that Claudius played no role in her first husband’s death and that he has no designs on her son’s life, but when she realizes that she has drunk poisoned wine, the horrible truth instantly becomes clear to her and her dying words try to warn Hamlet.

HORATIO

Horatio is Hamlet’s only close friend, his fellow student from Wittenberg and Hamlet’s model of self-possession and rational behavior. He is not “passion’s slave”; his volatile friend envies and admires Horatio’s perfect calm, which breaks briefly only when he realizes that Hamlet is about to die. But Hamlet dissuades Horatio from suicide by urging him to live and tell the world the full story, which only he will know.

Horatio is no yes-man or flatterer. He is quite ready to rebuke his royal friend when Hamlet is out of control. During the graveyard fight with Laertes he says sharply, “Good my lord, be quiet!” On other occasions his quiet wisdom is felt even when he says little. He is notably restrained when Hamlet exults after the play has destroyed Claudius’s composure. We sense that he knows Hamlet has botched an opportunity by letting his emotions get the better of him. When Hamlet muses on mortality in the graveyard, Horatio tells him he is dwelling “too curiously” on the morbid. He is also quietly shocked when Hamlet proudly relates how he arranged the deaths of Rosencrantz and Guildenstern.

Though Hamlet wants to believe the Ghost, Horatio is not so sure. He warns Hamlet about the danger of following it, and he proves to be right. He has no illusions about anyone. It is the cool Horatio, not the raging Ghost, whom Hamlet should have listened to.

POLONIUS

Polonius exemplifies the corruption of Claudius's court. He is an incurable snoop, cynical and amoral. He even spies on his own children. His suspicious nature spoils the blossoming love of Hamlet and Ophelia, and he sends his servant Reynaldo to keep an eye on Laertes in Paris, blackening Laertes's character if necessary in order to elicit information.

Polonius's judgment is poor. He cannot give up the idea that Ophelia's rejection has driven Hamlet mad, though Claudius quickly sees that this is nonsense and that Hamlet is dangerous. The duel of wits between Claudius and Hamlet goes completely over the old man's head.

Polonius loves the sound of his own voice. Vainly garrulous, he tries to control every situation. Gertrude tries to make him get to the point ("More matter with less art," she orders him tartly), but she should have saved her breath; he will not be silenced.

He has no real interest in the theater; he despises the actors, despite Hamlet's warning that they may have the last word on men like him: "After your death you were better have a bad epitaph than their ill report while you live." Though Polonius sees that Hamlet is behaving outrageously during the play, he fails to grasp what is really going on; he still thinks Hamlet is preoccupied with Ophelia.

Why does Hamlet seem to hate the relatively harmless old Polonius more than the man who has murdered his father and debauched his mother? We are left to wonder, though Polonius is certainly a vexing figure.

When he insists on eavesdropping on Gertrude and her son, urging her to be severe, he is, as usual, out of his depth, and the result is his death. Until he kills Polonius, Hamlet is gaining the upper hand over his real enemy, Claudius; but then the balance of power shifts against him. He treats the corpse with complete contempt. "I'll lug the guts into the neighbor room," he tells Gertrude, and when Rosencrantz and Guildenstern demand to know where Hamlet has hidden the body, he says sarcastically that its odor will eventually guide them.

LAERTES

His father's son, Laertes is a shallow playboy who has obviously not gone to Paris to study the questions that have drawn Hamlet and Horatio to Wittenberg. Polonius is proud of the boy, whatever his vices; Ophelia, though innocent and pious herself, is wise to him.

When he learns of his father's death, Laertes reacts in a flash, without anguished soliloquies. He wants revenge—at once. The contrast between him and Hamlet could hardly be more stark:

> TO HELL, ALLEGIANCE! VOWS TO THE BLACKEST DEVIL!
> CONSCIENCE AND GRACE TO THE PROFOUNDEST PIT!
> I DARE DAMNATION.

Laertes has no illusions about the diabolical nature of revenge, but he could not care less. He is not the man to admire a calm Horatio. He defies Gertrude's plea for him to be calm: "That drop of blood that's calm proclaims me bastard!" He is indeed "passion's slave," and he is proud of it.

And yet, at bottom, his fury is merely a distilled version of Hamlet's first response to the Ghost, when the prince vowed that the Ghost's command would live "all alone" in his mind, "unmixed with baser matter." But whereas Hamlet found himself unable to sustain an obsession with revenge, Laertes finds it natural. He would be willing "to cut [Hamlet's] throat i'th' church." And he is ready to stoop to treachery in order to get even. He is even more enraged when he sees Ophelia insane and then learns that she has drowned.

Even Laertes has his limits, though. When the plot to kill Hamlet with the poisoned foil is on the verge of being executed, he admits to himself, "And yet it is almost against my conscience."

"SWEETS TO THE SWEET: FAREWELL!"

Almost. Then, suddenly, everything goes wrong. The foils are exchanged, Laertes is fatally wounded, and the queen drinks the poisoned wine that was meant for Hamlet. In the ensuing uproar Laertes confesses everything, blames the king, and begs Hamlet for forgiveness, which is readily given.

In the end we, too, absolve and forgive Laertes. He has been cruelly wronged, tenderly cares for his poor sister, and, though used cynically by Claudius, has turned out to be a far better man than his father.

OPHELIA

Of all Shakespeare's heroines, the sweet Ophelia has the weakest personality. Her will is too unassertive to stand up to Polonius, her cruel and suspicious father, when he orders her to cease all contact with Hamlet immediately. She allows herself to be used to spy on Hamlet. He senses this and is infuriated by it.

Yet she always means well. There is not a speck of malice or cunning in her. Everyone in the corrupt court loves her for her purity and innocence. Gertrude hoped she would marry Hamlet, and even Claudius is touched by her madness and death (despite her apparent suicide, he orders the church to give her a normal funeral).

When Hamlet insults her, she really thinks he has gone mad. She remembers him as a model gentleman, courtier, scholar, and soldier, and cannot explain his violent change to her except as a baffling explosion of insanity. When, at the play, his taunts become downright obscene, she scolds him mildly, trying to insist on a little decency, but he ignores her objections. He is too angry to consider what she deserves.

The next time we see her, her mind has snapped. Her father has been slain, her brother is gone, and Hamlet has turned against her, She is alone and friendless. The furies of the men around her have destroyed her (she knows nothing of the Ghost and the murder, of course). No wonder she drowns herself.

Sent to England Hamlet escapes and returns to Denmark just in time to see Ophelia's funeral procession. This is his first notice of her death; he is shocked. His love for her comes flooding back. He vies with Laertes in extravagant professions of love for her, but he still fails to see his own role in her destruction. Though she is the most innocent victim of his tragic quest for revenge, he never reflects on what it has done to them both. Like Laertes he is willing to see the innocent destroyed along with the guilty. Masculine hatred consumes feminine love.

Like Horatio, but in a very different way, Ophelia is a measure of what Hamlet has become. If Horatio stands for the quality of reasonableness that Hamlet has forsaken in his pursuit of revenge, then Ophelia represents the innocence he is willing to sacrifice to the same evil purpose. Is his soul lost at the end? We are not told, and we sympathize with Horatio's final prayer for him; but it is a good question.

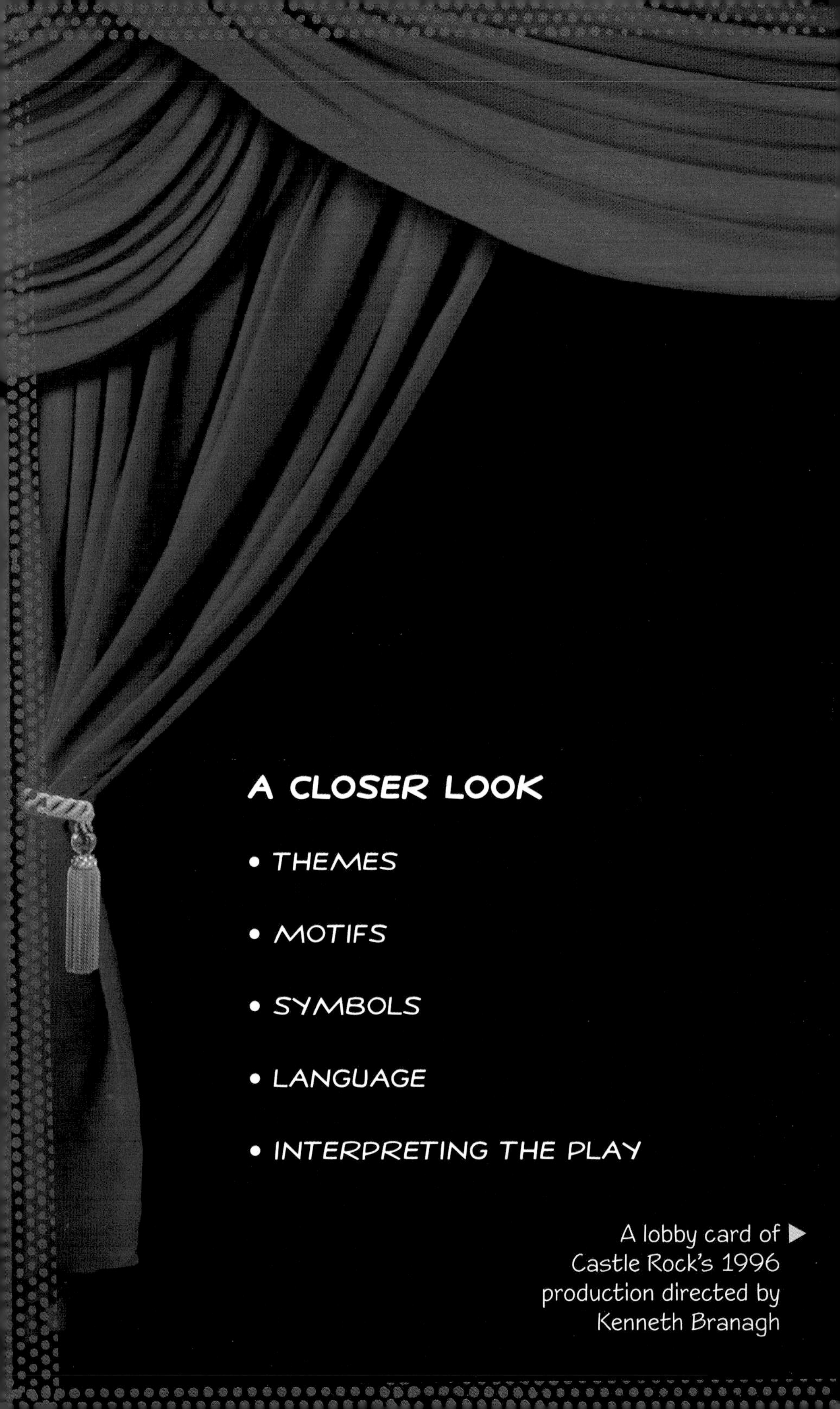

A CLOSER LOOK

- THEMES
- MOTIFS
- SYMBOLS
- LANGUAGE
- INTERPRETING THE PLAY

A lobby card of ▶
Castle Rock's 1996
production directed by
Kenneth Branagh

Chapter Three

CHAPTER THREE

A Closer Look

THEMES

THE CONSEQUENCES OF REVENGE

The chief theme of *Hamlet* is obviously revenge. The play explores the elusive difference between hating the sin and hating the sinner, between punishing and getting even. Hamlet hates his uncle even before learning that Claudius has murdered his father, an apparently simple fact that Hamlet feels he must prove before he proceeds to avenge it.

Hamlet's emotions are as complicated as they are powerful, and he has our full sympathy as he tries to consider every angle of this baffling task, which tests his immense intelligence. His own life may be at stake, and so is his immortal soul. The wrong answer may bring about his eternal damnation.

THE INEVITABILITY OF DEATH

The theme of revenge also involves the theme of death. From the Ghost's first appearance to the final scene, with such seemingly digressive episodes as the exhuming of Yorick's skull before Ophelia's burial, we are seldom allowed to forget it. Mortality pervades this play like no other. Denmark stinks with it. As Gertrude puts it, "All that lives must die,/Passing through nature to eternity."

That is the play's major premise. It receives many elaborations, such as Hamlet's morbid joke to Claudius that "a man may fish with the worm that hath eat of a king, and eat of the fish that hath fed of that worm," so that "a king may go a progress through the guts of a beggar." (We are apt to ask: Does he really have to tell us this?) Similarly he broods caustically on "the noble dust of Alexander" (the Great), which may have wound up stopping a hole in a beer-barrel, and likewise on "Imperious Caesar, dead and turned to clay."

THE AMBIGUITY OF RELIGIOUS DOCTRINES

Death, the final divorce of body and soul, brings us to the theme of religion. Four quick mentions of the university at Wittenberg, where Hamlet and Horatio have studied together, alert us that both young men must be well aware of the new doctrines of Protestantism that were born there. This is a superb instance of Shakespeare's tact: The disputes between Catholics and Protestants were an extremely sensitive subject in Elizabethan England, whose official church stood somewhere between the Pope and the Puritans, banning any explicit affirmation of purgatory.

Shakespeare evades this problem by referring only to Wittenberg, home of Martin Luther, and counting on his audience to pick up the associations. When the ambiguous Ghost says that its sins are being "purged" in fire, we are invited to infer, if we choose, that it has come from purgatory, but the Bard leaves that up to us. And when the Ghost complains that it has died without the sacraments, we again have to draw our own conclusions.

Shakespeare keeps playing on religious uncertainties of this sort, tantalizing us with "Thoughts beyond the reaches of our souls." After the play scene Hamlet finds his uncle on his knees, seemingly praying. Is this an apt moment to take his revenge? He considers that his own father died with his sins on his soul, and he reasons that if he kills Claudius now, repentant, Claudius may go to heaven. Full revenge would require killing him during the commission of his sins, thus sending him straight to hell. So Hamlet delays once more.

Critics have long debated whether Hamlet sincerely means what he says in this scene, or whether he is just making one more excuse for shirking a duty he shrinks from. With exquisite poise, Shakespeare leaves us in doubt again. But we may note that Hamlet sends Rosencrantz and Guildenstern to die like his father, without the final sacraments, and when Laertes curses him in the graveyard—"The devil take thy soul!"—he instantly retorts, "Thou prayest not well." True enough, but it amounts to the same prayer Hamlet has been saying as he seeks to damn his enemies.

Unlike the old Scandinavian tale from which it derives, *Hamlet* is so steeped in Christian language, concepts, and symbols that we can never disentangle it from them. It mentions or alludes to God, Jesus, Adam, Cain, Jeptha, King Herod, Saint Patrick, Saint Valentine, Original Sin, sin in general, angels, devils, the church, sacraments, Doomsday, the Last Trumpet, salvation, damnation, heaven, hell, purgatory, prayers, vows, oaths, curses, the immortal soul, miracles, prophecy, conscience, priesthood, the nunnery, divine providence, the mass, the requiem, hymns, the Christmas season, witchcraft, and more. Ophelia, always proper and pious, becomes even more religious in her madness.

In death, as Adam is told by God, man, made from dust, returns to dust—another thematic word in *Hamlet*. Man, the paragon of animals, angelic and godlike, now seems to Hamlet "this quintessence of dust," no longer a source of admiration and delight. Yet the play, at once deeply Christian and just as deeply baffling, never fully commits itself to either a Catholic or a Protestant position, leaving us to wonder where the ultimate truth lies.

MOTIFS

In his first soliloquy Hamlet reveals that he is revolted and disgusted by "all the uses of this world." The play keeps echoing his dark estimate of what he finally, on the verge of his own death, calls "this harsh world."

As he tells Polonius, in a more bantering vein, "To be honest, as this world goes, is to be one man picked out of ten thousand." Yet he sincerely means what he says.

Claudius, trying to repent for his own terrible sins, contrasts this world with the next one:

> IN THE CORRUPTED CURRENTS OF THIS WORLD,
> OFFENSE'S GILDED HAND MAY SHOVE BY JUSTICE,
> AND OFT 'TIS SEEN THE WICKED PRIZE ITSELF
> BUYS OUT THE LAW. BUT 'TIS NOT SO ABOVE. . . .

He is thinking specifically of himself. In this corrupt world, he is saying, the guilty rich man may bribe his way to power and success, just as he has done, even using the very crown he has stolen to buy off others, but it is otherwise in heaven, where hypocrisy is impossible and God sees the moral quality of our actions without their earthly disguises.

Others are also well aware of the double standards that prevail in this sinful world. The two gravediggers agree that Ophelia, who committed suicide, is being allowed a proper Christian funeral only because of her high social rank. Otherwise, one of these poor men remarks, she would have been buried in disgrace at the crossroads, like other suicides. The other concurs: "And the more pity that great folk should have countenance in this world to drown or hang themselves more than their even-Christen" (i.e., their fellow Christians). His protest may sound a little absurd, put this way, but he has a point.

That point is echoed by the pitiless priest who conducts the funeral. The way Ophelia died was "doubtful," he says, and only the king's decree has overruled normal church procedure for suicides ("great command o'ersways the order," as he says pithily).

Related to this is the motif of hypocrisy, which is signaled in various ways. One is the woman's vanity of cosmetics, "The harlot's cheek, beautied with plastering art," in Claudius's words when a remark of Polonius's happens to sting his conscience. Hamlet (quite unfairly) blames Ophelia for all the false pretenses of her gender: "I have heard of your paintings too, well enough: God hath given you one face, and you make yourselves another." His final comment on this subject is his mock order to Yorick's skull: "Now get you to my lady's chamber, and tell her, let her paint an inch thick, to this favor she must come." That is, no matter how much makeup she applies, she will end up with a face like Yorick's. (He says this before he knows that Ophelia is already dead.)

Against, or supplementing, the play's religious themes is its motif of classical learning from pagan antiquity. There are collections of both its historical and its mythological figures. The historical include Caesar and Alexander, of course, as well as Brutus, Nero, and sites such as the Roman Capitol, Mount Olympus, Pelion, and Ossa. The names *Claudius* and *Horatio* are Roman, too; Horatio, trying to kill himself, actually says he is "more an antique Roman than a Dane."

We also hear of many pagan gods: Jove (king of the gods); Hyperion, also called Phoebus (the sun-god); Mars (god of war); Hymen (god of marriage); Neptune (the sea-god); Hecate (goddess of witchcraft); Tellus (Earth's goddess); Vulcan (the gods' blacksmith); and the mighty Hercules, the horrid Cyclops, the grieving Niobe, and fearsome beasts such as the Nemean lion and the Hyrcanian tiger. The destruction of Troy, or Ilium, is recounted, too, as narrated by Virgil's Aeneas to Queen Dido, with recollections of the slaughter of King Priam by "the rugged Pyrrhus," son of Achilles, and the uncontrollable grief of Priam's piteous queen, Hecuba. The Trojan Horse merits a brief allusion. The Ghost also speaks of Lethe, the river of forgetfulness in Hades.

All this classical lore serves several purposes. It adds further volume and resonance to the play's rich language—in doing so, it also enlarges Hamlet's mental universe. It also cunningly distracts us from the Christian setting of Denmark, and it enables Hamlet to exalt his father in heroic terms, avoiding the fatal subject of the "foul crimes" for which the Ghost is being punished.

Another important motif in *Hamlet* is the relation between memory and purpose. The Ghost commands Hamlet, "Remember me," and Hamlet swears he will do so, erasing everything else from "the book and volume of my brain." But later, during his verbal assault on Gertrude, the Ghost has to return to remind him, "Do not forget," chiding him for "thy almost blunted purpose." In the play scene, the Player King (whose speeches make shrewd comments on the "real" action of the play), observes:

PURPOSE IS BUT THE SLAVE TO MEMORY,
OF VIOLENT BIRTH, BUT POOR VALIDITY.

His thought is echoed when Claudius says to Laertes that "love is begun by time," and that "time qualifies the spark and fire of it." If we fail to act

"LIKE NIOBE, ALL TEARS."

quickly on our love, such as by taking revenge in the heat of passion, time may dissipate our will to do so. He is talking about Laertes, but of course these words also (though Claudius does not realize it) describe Hamlet, whose initial eagerness to take revenge has long since faded.

SYMBOLS

Denmark's evil is symbolized by the poison Claudius chooses for his murders, which turns out to be an evil he is unable to control. He finally manages to arrange Hamlet's death, but he himself dies of poison, too, along with Gertrude and Laertes. Again and again the play shows men unable to control their passions and the natural consequences of their actions. The plot is so beautifully constructed that even its accidents always seem as real and lifelike as its most humanly motivated events. This play truly holds the mirror up to nature.

There are also several metaphorical references to poison and venom. Slander and calumny (hurtful misrepresentations) are said to be poisonous in their effects. Hamlet is said (no doubt falsely, since we have only Claudius's word for it) to be "envenomed" with envy of Laertes; he assures the king that the actors merely "poison in jest."

Another figurative form of poison is drunkenness. In the first scene in which he appears, Claudius drinks, as he loves to do, to the sound of cannons roaring. Hamlet finds this disgusting. He welcomes Horatio to Elsinore with the wry promise, "We'll teach you to drink deep ere you depart." That night, as they await the Ghost, they hear the cannons roar again. Hamlet explains that this is a Danish custom, albeit one he considers "more honored in the breach than the observance." This "heavy-headed revel," he says, has earned the Danes a "swinish" international reputation as a country of drunkards. There is further evidence of Claudius's addiction to drink later in the play, but the baneful tradition clearly did not begin with him; presumably Hamlet's father had his share in it, too.

Denmark's sins are further conveyed to us by Shakespeare's rich imagery of disease and malady. Terms such as *sick*, *disease*, *infection*, *ulcer* (or *imposthume*), *pleurisy*, *apoplexed*, *leprous*, *corruption*, *cicatrice* (scar), and *hectic* (fever) recur time and again. The aging king of Norway, uncle of Fortinbras, is "bedrid"; corpses are "rotten," "pocky" (syphilitic), and foul-smelling. "How long will a man lie in the earth ere he rot?" Hamlet asks the gravedigger. Joking about his pretended madness, he says, "My wit's diseased." The language of pathology and medicine is offset by the occasional use of such terms as *health* and *wholesome*, but our chief and most powerful impression is of a deeply diseased world typified by Denmark, where "something is rotten."

All this language thickens our sense of the play's inclusive reality. It seeks to deal comprehensively, if darkly, with all we know of human experience and its unfathomable mysteries.

THERE ARE MORE THINGS IN
HEAVEN AND EARTH, HORATIO,
THAN ARE DREAMT OF IN YOUR PHILOSOPHY.

Dreams themselves are part of this reality. Hamlet says, "O God, I could be bounded in a nutshell and count myself a king of infinite space, were it not that I have bad dreams" (Hamlet loves the term *infinite*: He can dream of infinite space, man is infinite in faculties, Yorick was a fellow of infinite jest) and "To sleep, perchance to dream."

LANGUAGE

Aside from the King James translation of the Bible, no work has had remotely as powerful an impact on the English language as *Hamlet*. Dozens of its lines and phrases are familiar to educated readers. Here is a brief sampling:

"A little more than kin, and less than kind." "Hyperion to a satyr." "The primrose path." "The apparel oft proclaims the man." "Neither a borrower nor a lender be." "To thine own self be true." "A custom more honored in the breach than the observance." "Murder most foul." "One may smile, and smile, and be a villain." "Wild and whirling words." "There are more things in heaven and earth, Horatio, than are dreamt of in your philosophy." "An antic disposition." "The time is out of joint." "By indirections find directions out." "Brevity is the soul of wit." "More matter, with less art." "Though this be madness, yet there is method in it." "The paragon of animals." "Caviar to the general." "What's Hecuba to him, or he to Hecuba?" "The play's the thing." "To be or not to be: that is the question." "The slings and arrows of outrageous fortune." "To sleep, perchance to dream; ay, there's the rub." "The pangs of despised love." "The undiscovered country from whose bourn no traveler returns." "Thus conscience does make cowards of us all." "Enterprises of great pith and moment." "Get thee to a nunnery. Why wouldst thou be a breeder of sinners?" "God hath given you one face, and you make yourselves another." "The glass of fashion, and the mold of form."

"Trippingly on the tongue." "It out-Herods Herod." "Suit the action to the word, the word to the action." "To hold, as it were, the mirror up to nature." "Passion's slave." "The lady doth protest too much, methinks." "Very like a whale." "The very witching time of night." "I will speak daggers to her, but use none." "A king of shreds and patches." "I must be cruel, only to be kind." "Hoist with his own petar." "When sorrows come, they come not single spies, but in battalions." "O, you must wear your rue with a difference." "Alas, poor Yorick! I knew him, Horatio." "Sweets to the sweet!" "There's a divinity that shapes our ends, rough-hew them how we will." "Yeoman's service." "A hit, a very palpable hit." "Absent thee from felicity a while." "The rest is silence." "Good night, sweet prince, and flights of angels sing thee to thy rest."

The English language is simply unimaginable without Shakespeare's contribution to it, most of all in *Hamlet*. All literate speakers of the English tongue are in his debt.

A ludicrous legend has grown up that Shakespeare was hardly educated, a spontaneous natural genius with no need of schooling—that he had, in Ben Jonson's words, "small Latin and less Greek." (John Milton likewise has Shakespeare "warbling his native woodnotes wild.")

A book that appeared in 1947, *Shakespeare's Use of the Arts of Language*, by a nun named Sister Miriam Joseph, C.S.C., should have quashed forever any notion that the Bard was unbookish. This staggering work of scholarship demonstrated his intimacy with hundreds of technical terms from classical and Renaissance rhetoric: not only those most of us are still familiar with, such as *simile*, *metaphor*, *antithesis*, *paradox*, and the like, but such little-known terms as *brachylogia*, *zeugma*, *anamnesis*, *epizeuxis*, *pysma*, *diasyrmus*, *tmesis*, and many, many more. The book gives copious examples of all these phrases from Shakespeare's plays.

Not only did Shakespeare know his business in the theater; he was

BY AND BY IS EASILY SAID

also a literary artist and poet of enormous sophistication in all the uses of language. Today the very term *rhetoric* sounds pejorative to us; it suggests empty, inflated, insincere speech—"mere" rhetoric, as we say, the debased language of advertising and politics. But in Shakespeare's day, rhetoric, the serious art of persuasion, was a highly developed and respectable field of study. Aristotle, Cicero, and other noted scholars had written important books about it.

Such men, like Shakespeare himself, understood that the kind of plain language we prize today is itself only one form of rhetoric, and not necessarily the best. They could also enjoy the most elaborate uses of language, and they would have been puzzled by the modern prejudice in favor of simplicity. Had not God given man all the rich resources of his mind and tongue to be used and delighted in?

A *Hamlet* written in "basic" English would not be *Hamlet*. Its matchless rhetoric makes it what it is: the play that millions of readers and spectators have always loved. Simplification would not improve it but utterly destroy it.

In one respect *Hamlet* departs stylistically from Shakespeare's earlier plays. It adopts a striking mannerism: the slightly redundant doubling of synonyms connected by the word *and*, often using words of both Latin and Anglo-Saxon derivation that mean nearly the same thing. In the first act alone we find these phrases:

"sensible and true avouch," "strict and most observant watch," "the most high and palmy state of Rome," "the extravagant and erring spirit," "impotent and bedrid," "an understanding simple and unschooled," "gentle and unforced accord," "in the dead waste and middle of the night," "oppressed and fear-surprised eyes," "a fashion and a toy in blood," "the perfume and suppliance of a minute," "the safety and the health of this whole state," "the voice and yielding of that body," "his particular act and place," "the shot and danger of desire," "the morn and liquid dew of youth," "a puffed and reckless libertine," "most free and bounteous," "sanctified and pious bawds," "traduced and taxed of other nations," "the pith and marrow of our attribute," "the pales and forts of reason," "ponderous and marble jaws." "sulfurous and tormenting flames," "the natural gates and alleys of the body," "the thin and wholesome blood," "with vile and loathsome crust," "within the book and volume of my brain," "wild and whirling words," and "love and friending."

INTERPRETING THE PLAY

HAMLET AND THE CRITICS

Serious criticism and scholarship of the play began in the middle of the eighteenth century. The extremely versatile English writer Samuel Johnson—poet, critic, novelist, lexicographer, scholar, editor, and wit—singled out Hamlet as the greatest of Shakespeare's plays for its sheer "variety" and abundance of character and incident.

Meanwhile Shakespeare, previously almost unknown outside England, was becoming the rage in Germany, where another literary giant, Johann Wolfgang von Goethe became one of his great advocates. Goethe, too, was fascinated by Hamlet, both the character and the play. He argued that Hamlet was too "delicate" and "effeminate" to pursue the violent mission of revenge, an argument also taken up by another great English poet and critic, Samuel Taylor Coleridge.

At the beginning of the twentieth century, Andrew Cecil Bradley, the most influential of all Shakespeare critics, rejected this view of Hamlet as a weakling in his 1904 classic, *Shakespearean Tragedy*. Bradley's insight into the nature of Shakespeare's tragedies was profound. Their premise, he held, is that "men may set off a course of events which they can neither calculate nor control," bringing destruction both on themselves and on their societies.

As for Hamlet, Bradley's diagnosis was more open to dispute. He argued against Goethe and Coleridge that Hamlet is a man quite capable of action—he faces the Ghost with great courage, he kills Polonius in a flash, he boards an attacking pirate ship without hesitation, he does not shrink from fighting Laertes—but his will is paralyzed by "melancholy," or emotional depression, brought on by two severe shocks: his father's sudden death and his mother's quick remarriage to the uncle he despises.

Debate over the play, centering on the prince's character and its putative flaws, continued in the twentieth century. The poet and critic T. S. Eliot boldly declared *Hamlet* "most certainly an artistic failure" because, he said, the hero's emotions are "in excess of the facts as they appear"; Shakespeare is unable to justify his hero's overwhelming passion. Eliot's argument caused much comment in its day, but few critics have agreed that the play fails.

John Dover Wilson's 1935 book, *What Happens in Hamlet*, offered a close scene-by-scene analysis of the play and had much effect on how it was staged and acted for some years. Sigmund Freud held a psychoanalytical view of Hamlet that also had a time of popularity: He argued that the prince is the victim of an Oedipus complex that gives him a guilty sympathy with Claudius and inhibits him from taking revenge. As Freud saw it, Hamlet had a secret wish to kill his father and sleep with his mother, so he could not bring himself to kill the man who had only done what he wished to do. Today this view may seem outlandish and dated, but as developed by Freud's English disciple Ernest Jones in his 1949 book *Hamlet and Oedipus*, it has an odd plausibility. Laurence Olivier adopted the psychoanalytic view (as well as some of Dover Wilson's ideas) in his 1948 film of the play.

In his posthumous 1951 book *The Meaning of Shakespeare*, Harold Clarke Goddard rejected the whole premise of nearly all previous *Hamlet* criticism. Goddard argued that Hamlet's delay is due to his conscience: He knows that the Ghost's demand for revenge is evil. This argument was echoed in John Vyvyan's 1959 book *The Shakespearean Ethic*, which contended that the Ghost is a typical Shakespearean seducer, inciting violence like Cassius in *Julius Caesar*, Iago in *Othello*, and the Weird Sisters in *Macbeth*. Eleanor Prosser took this view even further in her powerful 1967 study *Hamlet and Revenge*. Goddard's thesis has also been taken up with enthusiasm by such critics as L. C. Knights, Norman Rabkin, and Harold Bloom.

Later studies, such as those of Northrop Frye and Stephen Booth, have inclined back toward the older view that revenge is Hamlet's moral duty. Maynard Mack, in his highly regarded essay "The World of *Hamlet*," sees the play as taking place in a realm of ultimate and irresolvable mystery, where the great questions the prince faces defy final answers.

Chronology

1564	William Shakespeare is born on April 23 in Stratford-upon-Avon, England
1578–1582	Span of Shakespeare's "Lost Years," covering the time between leaving school and marrying Anne Hathaway of Stratford
1582	At age eighteen Shakespeare marries Anne Hathaway, age twenty-six, on November 28
1583	Susanna Shakespeare, William and Anne's first child, is born in May, six months after the wedding
1584	Birth of twins Hamnet and Judith Shakespeare
1585–1592	Shakespeare leaves his family in Stratford to become an actor and playwright in a London theater company
1587	Public beheading of Mary Queen of Scots
1593–94	The Bubonic (Black) Plague closes theaters in London
1594–96	As a leading playwright, Shakespeare creates some of his most popular work, including *A Midsummer Night's Dream* and *Romeo and Juliet*
1596	Hamnet Shakespeare dies in August at age eleven, possibly of plague

1596–97 *The Merchant of Venice* and *Henry IV, Part One* most likely are written

1599 The Globe Theater opens

1600 *Julius Caesar* is first performed at the Globe

1600–01 *Hamlet* is believed to have been written

1601–02 *Twelfth Night* is probably composed

1603 Queen Elizabeth dies; Scottish king James VI succeeds her and becomes England's James I

1604 Shakespeare pens *Othello*

1605 *Macbeth* is composed

1608–1610 London's theaters are forced to close when the plague returns and kills an estimated 33,000 people

1611 *The Tempest* is written

1613 The Globe Theater is destroyed by fire

1614 Reopening of the Globe

1616 Shakespeare dies on April 23

1623 Anne Hathaway, Shakespeare's widow, dies; a collection of Shakespeare's plays, known as the First Folio, is published

Source Notes

p. 84, par. 1, The phrase "as opaque as life's" comes from an article, "To Man From Mankind's Heart," in *Time* magazine, July 4, 1960 and can be read at http://www.time.com/time/magazine/article/0,9171,869555-9,00.html

p. 109, par. 3, Sister Miriam Joseph. *Shakespeare's Use of the Arts of* Language. (Philadelphia: Paul Dry Books, 2005).This classic 1947 work is back in print and remains an invaluable guide for students of rhetoric as well as of Shakespeare.

p. 112, par. 2, Bradley, A.C. *Shakespearean Tragedy.* (New York: Penguin, 1991). Bradley's lectures on *Hamlet*, *Othello*, *King Lear*, and *Macbeth* have gone back to press many times in the past century and have been enjoyed by generations of Shakespeare enthusiasts.

p. 112, par. 4, Eliot wrote "Hamlet and His Problems" in a collection titled *The Sacred Wood: Essays on Poetry and Criticism,* published in 1922. The essay can be read at http://www.bartleby.com/200/sw9.html

p. 113, par. 1, Wilson, John Dover. *What Happens in Hamlet*. (New York: Cambridge University Press, 1951).

p. 113, par. 1, Jones, Ernest. *Hamlet and Oedipus*. (New York: Norton, 1976). As the book's cover notes, this is "a classic study in psychoanalytic criticism."

p. 113, par. 1, Laurence Olivier's black-and-white film, which Olivier both starred in and directed, won the 1948 Academy Awards for best film, best actor, best costume design, and best art direction. This heroic, athletic prince may not be the subtlest Hamlet, but he is unforgettable.

p. 113, par. 2, Goddard, Harold C. *The Meaning of Shakespeare*. (Chicago: University of Chicago Press, 1951). Profound studies of the plays, written in a simple, warm, non-academic style. Goddard finds imaginative patterns other commentators have missed.

p. 113, par. 2, Vyvyan, John. *The Shakespearean Ethic*. (New York: Barnes and Noble, 1968).

p. 113, par. 2, Prosser, Eleanor. *Hamlet and Revenge*. (Palo Alto, CA: Stanford University Press, 1977). This is a highly stimulating challenge to traditional interpretations of *Hamlet*.

p. 113, par. 3, Frye, Northrup. *Northrup Frye on Shakespeare*. (New Haven, CT: Yale University Press, 1988).

A Shakespeare Glossary

The student should not try to memorize these, but only refer to them as needed. We can never stress enough that the best way to learn Shakespeare's language is simply to *hear* it—to hear it spoken well by good actors. After all, small children master every language on earth through their ears, without studying dictionaries, and we should master Shakespeare, as much as possible, the same way.

addition —a name or title (knight, duke, duchess, king, etc.)
admire —to marvel
affect —to like or love; to be attracted to
an —if ("An I tell you that, I'll be hanged.")
approve —to prove or confirm
attend —to pay attention
belike —probably
beseech —to beg or request
betimes —soon; early
bondman —a slave
bootless —futile; useless; in vain
broil —a battle
charge —expense, responsibility; to command or accuse
clepe, clept —to name; named
common —of the common people; below the nobility
conceit —imagination
condition —social rank; quality
countenance —face; appearance; favor
cousin —a relative
cry you mercy —beg your pardon
curious —careful; attentive to detail
dear —expensive
discourse —to converse; conversation
discover —to reveal or uncover
dispatch —to speed or hurry; to send; to kill
doubt —to suspect

entreat —to beg or appeal
envy —to hate or resent; hatred; resentment
ere —before
ever, e'er —always
eyne —eyes
fain —gladly
fare —to eat; to prosper
favor —face, privilege
fellow —a peer or equal
filial —of a child toward its parent
fine —an end; in fine = in sum
fond —foolish
fool —a darling
genius —a good or evil spirit
gentle —well-bred; not common;
gentleman —one whose labor was done by servants (Note: to call someone a *gentleman* was not a mere compliment on his manners; it meant that he was above the common people.)
gentles —people of quality
get —to beget (a child)
go to —"go on"; "come off it"
go we —let us go
haply —perhaps
happily —by chance; fortunately
hard by —nearby
heavy —sad or serious
husbandry —thrift; economy
instant —immediate
kind— one's nature; species
knave— a villain; a poor man
lady— a woman of high social rank (Note: *lady* was not a synonym for *woman* or *polite woman*; it was not a compliment, but, like *gentleman*, simply a word referring to one's actual legal status in society.)
leave — permission; "take my leave" = depart (with permission)
lief, lieve —"I had as lief" = I would just as soon; I would rather
like —to please; "it likes me not" = it is disagreeable to me

livery —the uniform of a nobleman's servants; emblem
mark —notice; pay attention
morrow —morning
needs —necessarily
nice —too fussy or fastidious
owe —to own
passing —very
peculiar —individual; exclusive
privy —private; secret
proper —handsome; one's very own ("his proper son")
protest —to insist or declare
quite —completely
require —request
several —different, various;
severally —separately
sirrah —a term used to address social inferiors
sooth —truth
state —condition; social rank
still —always; persistently
success —result(s)
surfeit —fullness
touching —concerning; about; as for
translate —to transform
unfold —to disclose
villain —a low or evil person; originally, a peasant
voice —a vote; consent; approval
vouchsafe —to confide or grant
vulgar —common
want —to lack
weeds —clothing
what ho —"hello, there!"
wherefore —why
wit —intelligence; sanity
withal —moreover; nevertheless
without —outside
would —wish

Suggested Essay Topics

1. Compare the ways in which Hamlet, Laertes, and Fortinbras react to their fathers' violent deaths.

2. Discuss the religious background of the play.

3. Gertrude, Hamlet's mother, has traditionally been seen as a stupid, passive, sensual woman. Is this judgment fair to her?

4. Horatio is Hamlet's only close friend. What does this say about both of them?

Testing Your Memory

1. What country is threatening to invade Denmark?
   a) England; b) Norway; c) Poland; d) Germany.
2. Where have Hamlet and Horatio gone to school?
   a) Paris; b) Wittenberg; c) Oxford; d) Cambridge.
3. Why does Polonius send Reynaldo to Paris?
   a) To attend the university; b) To borrow money; c) To follow Hamlet; d) To spy on Laertes.
4. What vice are the Danes notorious for?
   a) drunkenness; b) quarreling; c) gambling; d) smoking.
5. At what time of day does the Ghost say he was murdered?
   a) dawn; b) afternoon; c) evening; d) midnight.
6. Whom do the king and queen ask to get to the bottom of Hamlet's strange behavior?
   a) Ophelia; b) Horatio; c) Laertes; d) Rosencrantz and Guildenstern.
7. What fictional woman does the First Player weep for?
   a) Helen of Troy; b) Andromache; c) Hecuba; d) Penelope.
8. What is the "undiscovered country" to which Hamlet refers?
   a) America; b) death; c) purgatory; d) ignorance.
9. How do Claudius and Gertrude react to the news that Hamlet wants them to attend a play?
   a) They welcome it as evidence that he is normal again; b) They are dismayed; c) Gertrude is glad, but Claudius is suspicious; d) They want to know more about the play.
10. Where does Hamlet tell Ophelia to go?
    a) home; b) to hell; c) to a nunnery; d) to Paris.
11. How does Ophelia take Hamlet's harsh language to her?
    a) It makes her furious; b) She is mystified; c) It convinces her that he is really insane; d) She prays for him.
12. What is the purpose of acting, according to Hamlet?

a) To imitate nature; b) To win awards; c) To earn a profit; d) To inspire social reform.

13. What quality does Hamlet most admire in Horatio?

a) His intelligence; b) His scholarship; c) His courage; d) His patience.

14. What is the actual title of the play Hamlet calls *The Mousetrap*?

a) *The Revenger's Tragedy*; b) *The Murder of Gonzago*; c) *Oedipus Rex*; d) *The Fall of Troy*.

15. When Hamlet finds Claudius on his knees, what reason does he give for sparing his life?

a) He is afraid of sending him to heaven; b) There has been too much bloodshed already; c) He wants to give him another chance; d) He hopes Laertes will kill him.

16. Why is Hamlet reluctant to see his mother alone?

a) He fears a scolding; b) He is tempted to kill her; c) She knows about the murder of his father; d) He will have to tell her the full truth about Claudius.

17. Where is Hamlet going when the pirates capture him?

a) He is fleeing Claudius; b) He is being sent to England; c) He is returning to Wittenberg; d) He is on his way to meet Fortinbras.

18. What was the name of the court jester Hamlet knew as a child?

a) Yorick; b) Osric; c) Benedick; d) Dogberry.

19. Why would Ophelia be denied a normal funeral?

a) Because of the king's command; b) Because of her family's influence; c) Because her death may have been a suicide; d) Because of her association with Hamlet.

20. Who ultimately becomes king of Denmark?

a) Horatio; b) Laertes; c) Fortinbras; d) Donalbain.

Answer Key

1.b; 2.b; 3.d; 4.a; 5.b; 6.d; 7.c; 8.b; 9.a; 10.c; 11.c;
12.a; 13.d; 14.b; 15.a; 16.b; 17.b; 18.a; 19.c; 20.c

Further Information

BOOKS

Ackroyd, Peter.*Shakespeare: The Biography*. New York: Nan A. Talese, 2005.

Dunton-Downer, Leslie, and Alan Riding. *The Essential Shakespeare Handbook*. New York, Dorling-Kindersley, 2004.

Folger Shakespeare Library *Hamlet*. New York: Washington Square Press, 2004.

Manga Shakespeare series. *Hamlet*. New York: Harry N. Abrams/ Amulet, 2007.

WEB SITES

Absolute Shakespeare is a resource for the Bard's plays, sonnets, and poems and includes summaries, quotes, films, trivia, and more.
http://absoluteshakespeare.com

Play Shakespeare: The Ultimate Free Shakespeare Resource features all the play texts with an online glossary, reviews, a discussion forum, and links to festivals worldwide.
http://www.playshakespeare.com

William Shakespeare Info: *Hamlet* provides a vast collection of links related to the specific play, as well as articles about Shakespeare's life, world, and work.
http://www.william-shakespeare.info/shakespeare-play-hamlet.htm

FILMS

Hamlet, directed by Laurence Olivier; with Olivier as Hamlet, 1948.

Hamlet, Broadway production starring Richard Burton, videotaped in 1964 and transferred to DVD.

Hamlet, BBC production; with Derek Jacobi as Hamlet and Patrick Stewart as Claudius, 1980.

Hamlet, directed by Franco Zeffirelli; with Mel Gibson as Hamlet and Helena Bonham Carter as Ophelia, 1990.

William Shakespeare's Hamlet, directed by Kenneth Branagh; with Branagh as Hamlet, Derek Jacobi as Claudius, and Kate Winslet as Ophelia, 1996.

Hamlet 2000, adapted for the screen and directed by Michael Almereyda; with Ethan Hawke as Hamlet, Julia Stiles as Ophelia, and Bill Murray as Polonius, 2000.

AUDIO BOOK

Hamlet(Arkangel Shakespeare), BBC Audiobooks America; performed by Simon Russell Beale, Imogen Stubbs, and the Arkangel cast.

RECORDINGS

John Gielgud, widely regarded as the greatest Hamlet of the twentieth century, left two recordings of the play, one a short version for radio, the other unabridged. He was famed for his vocal elegance and beauty: Many called him "the world's greatest actor from the neck up."

Paul Scofield, an actor of rare depth, conveys the prince's sensitivity and anguish as few others have. The beauty of his voice rivals Gielgud's.

Bibliography

General Commentary

Bate, Jonathan, and Eric Rasmussen, eds. *William Shakespeare Complete Works (Modern Library)*. New York: Random House, 2007.

Bloom, Harold. *Shakespeare: The Invention of the Human*. New York: Riverhead Books,1998.

Garber, Marjorie. *Shakespeare After All*. New York: Pantheon, 2004.

Goddard, Harold C. *The Meaning of Shakespeare*. Chicago: University of Chicago Press, 1951.

Traversi, D. L. *An Approach to Shakespeare*. Palo Alto, CA: Stanford University Press, 1957.

Van Doren, Mark. *Shakespeare*. Garden City, NY: Doubleday, 1939.

Biography

Burgess, Anthony. *Shakespeare*. New York: Alfred A. Knopf, 1970.

Chute, Marchette. *Shakespeare of London*. New York: Dutton, 1949.

Greenblatt, Stephen. *Will in the World: How Shakespeare Became Shakespeare*. New York: W. W. Norton & Company, 2004.

Honan, Park. *Shakespeare: A Life*. New York: Oxford University Press, 1998.

Schoenbaum, Samuel. *William Shakespeare: A Documentary Life*. New York: Oxford University Press, 1975.

———. *William Shakespeare: Records and Images*. New York: Oxford University Press, 1981.

Index

Page numbers in **boldface** are illustrations.

About the Author

Joseph Sobran is the author of several books, including *Alias Shakespeare* (1997). He lives in northern Virginia.